BALTIC SEA CRUISES
2019-20

Volume 2 – Saint Petersburg to Warnemunde

CONTENTS

INTRODUCTION

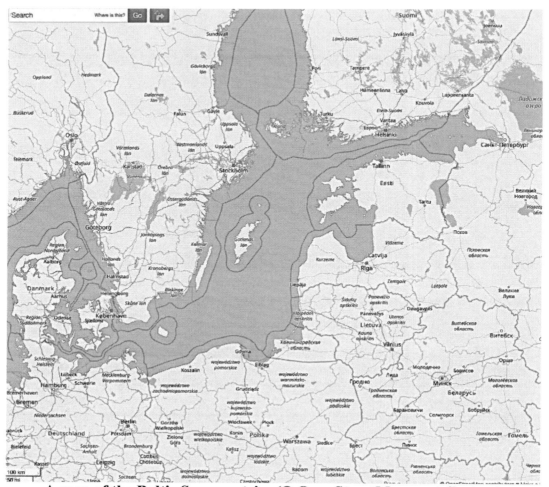

A map of the Baltic Sea countries (© OpenStreetMap contributors)

This is Volume 2 of a book that is a new concept emerging from several successful versions of my single volume title <u>Cruising the Baltic Sea</u> that I first wrote for Kindle in early 2015. Today Amazon publishes this book in paperback 8.5 x 11 inch format, both in standard black and white as well as a deluxe color edition, updated every other year. As the years have gone by, I have found that readers want more and more detailed information, photos and maps. But Amazon has size limits as to what can be published in a single book. Thus to accommodate requests for more detailed information, this is the first edition of a three volume set that enables the expansion of text, maps and photographs. In this new series I am able to expand the text by adding additional material on the geography and history of the Baltic Sea, enlarging each of the chapters on the ports of call to include more details about each location as well as limited, but specific dining and shopping information. I have also added numerous lesser ports of call, especially those around the Gulf of Bothnia that are visited by the smaller cruise ships, most often representing the higher end companies. I also included a transit through the Kiel Canal of Germany since many cruises on smaller or medium size vessels that begin or terminate in England or The

Netherlands use the canal for entering or departing the Baltic Sea. Of course not all cruise itineraries include every one of the ports of call listed in this book, but I have managed to include all possible Baltic destinations.

The popularity of the Baltic Sea has grown each year and today it is one of Europe's most popular cruise destinations. Summer in the Baltic Sea of northern Europe is a delightful season, especially for anyone who loves cool weather, as there are few days that could be called hot. The days are long, especially between mid-June and the end of July, and the farther north one travels they increase in length. In places like Saint Petersburg, Helsinki and Stockholm the days are up to 19 hours in length and the farther north one goes, they are even longer. Daylight hours will reach their maximum above the Arctic Circle to where there are approximately six weeks of total daylight. The Gulf of Bothnia, that long arm Baltic Sea reaches almost to the Arctic Circle and in ports such as Luela, Sweden or Kemi, Finland you will have almost a full 24 hours of daylight in June. In the major ports of Stockholm, Helsinki, Saint Petersburg and Tallinn the maximum daylight during this period is around 21-hours.

This region is one of the most popular venues for cruise ships, and all the major lines offer itineraries that vary from one to as much as two weeks. Some more up market cruise lines using smaller ships also include the Gulf of Bothnia on their longer Baltic Sea cruises. The highlight of any Baltic Sea cruise is the visit to Saint Petersburg, Russia. Some of the more upmarket cruise lines stay in port for as long as three days. Apart from visiting Saint Petersburg, all of the other Baltic ports are rich in historic sites and offer distinctive cultures presented in spotlessly clean settings, thus making for a grand tour that has become one of the most enticing in the cruise industry.

The main purpose of this three-volume set is to introduce you to the individual ports of call and the countries they represent. It will provide you with background information to help you better understand the places you will be visiting. To best appreciate one's surroundings, it is always advantageous to know something about the geography, history, social life and customs and major sites. Yet so many cruisers do not read up on the ports or countries they are visiting, and as a result they miss so much of the true value of international travel. The better informed the traveler is, the more rewarding the experience of visiting new places.

In this new series, I have included select recommendations as to my favorite restaurants where you will experience local cuisine. I have also added information regarding shopping for the major ports of call. I do include select hotel information for Copenhagen and Stockholm, as these two cities are the starting or ending points for the majority of Baltic Sea cruises with the exception of those that originate outside of the region in either Amsterdam, London or one of the English Channel ports of the United Kingdom. But I must advise that this is not a guidebook similar to what you can find in a bookstore travel section. The aim is not to provide hotel, restaurant and shopping detail as a primary focus, along with suggested walks or driving routes. When you are on a cruise, you will generally only have eight to 10 hours in port, sometimes even less. Therefore, this book is designed to make sure you can maximize your visit and see and experience as much as possible. The main focus is upon helping you to plan an itinerary or select among the ship's tour offerings with enough background to make the best choice possible. This will maximize your understanding and enjoyment of the ports of call on your itinerary. If you need the finite detail of a guidebook then I highly recommend that you look into publications by either Frommer of Fyodor.

The region of the Baltic Sea is one of the most beautiful and historic parts of Europe. Settlement dates back to before historic record keeping. Most visitors have heard or read stories about the Vikings who spread outward from the western margins of the Baltic Sea and terrorized the more sedentary peoples of the British Isles and the western coastal margins of Europe clear down to the Mediterranean. But few realize that Vikings also were great colonizers. Russia owes its very existence as a European society to early Viking settlers who pushed inland, utilizing rivers as a means of settling the vast interior forests and steppes. And Vikings were responsible for the settlement of Iceland, Greenland and even for a brief time the shores of what is now Newfoundland in Canada.

The Germanic tribes also played a major role in the development of this region, and their cultural impact has been very profound in historic times. Likewise, the Poles, and the Lithuanian people also expanded their nations and once dominated not only their neighboring peoples in the greater Baltic region, but extended their rule as far south as the Black Sea. During the middle ages, the Hanseatic League played a major role in the establishment of trade routes and port cities all around the margins of the Baltic Sea. And their architectural impact is virtually impossible to overlook in many Baltic ports.

Today with the breakup of the Soviet Union, the nations of the Baltic Sea are finally able to trade and interact with one another on a level that has been absent for nearly a century. Most of the Baltic nations have joined the European Union, thus giving them a unity of purpose with regard to trade and economic development. Yet the Western news media constantly warns of danger from Russian expansionism that could threaten the Baltic Sea region. Such factors will be brought out in several of the chapters to help you in asking important questions or looking for telltale signs of the political climate of the Baltic Sea, thus expanding your personal knowledge. Travel around the sea is no longer hindered by lengthy border crossings with the exception of entering Russia where the visa issue still is a factor to contend with for the majority of visitors. In Russia today tourism has come to play an important role in its economic development and its relationships with other nations bordering the Baltic Sea.

Most of the capital cities of the nations bordering the Baltic Sea are coastal ports with the exception of Germany, Poland, Russia and Lithuania. But in each case, the capital cities, which are located inland, have close ties to the ports on the Baltic Sea that are vital to national commerce.

This three volume book is designed to introduce the reader to the major cities of the Baltic Sea, with the inclusion of Berlin, capital of Germany because it is so closely associated with its coastal port of Warnemunde-Rostock where the majority of cruise lines stop and provide tours into the capital.

Although the author has written a specific book for those venturing to the city of Saint Petersburg, much of that text is included in this volume because it is such an important Baltic Sea port city and has played such an important role in the history of the region since its inception. For cruises around the Baltic Sea, Saint Petersburg is always the major highlight.

The content is organized into three volumes to best provide all the detail readers have asked for. The series is organized as follows:

* Volume 1 – Basic cruise information, background geography and history, entry into the Baltic Sea via the Kiel Canal, ports of Copenhagen, Bornholm Island, Malmö, Borgholm, Visby, Stockholm, Helsinki.

* Volume 2 – Saint Petersburg, Tallinn, Riga, Klaipedia, Gdansk, Warnemunde-Rostock.

* Volume 3 – Ports around the Gulf of Bothnia, including; * Sundsvall, Luleå, Kemi, Oulu, Vaasa, Marienham, Turku

If after reading this book you still have questions about any particular port or aspect of the region, you can contact me either through my web page, which is www.doctorlew.com or on Facebook. I will be only to pleased to respond. It is important to me to see that my readers maximize their knowledge of the Baltic Sea region before taking their cruise. This is a region that is so diverse, unlike the Mediterranean, and there is a lot to learn about the lands and peoples.

Dr. Lew Deitch,
January 2019

TIPS FOR CRUISING THE BALTIC SEA

Almost all major cruise lines offer summertime Baltic Sea itineraries. These cruise lines vary in price and of course in the levels of quality service and cuisine being offered. Most of the itineraries are very similar with the major ports of Copenhagen, Stockholm, Helsinki, St. Petersburg and Tallinn included in the one week cruises. Longer itineraries may include Warnemunde/Rostock, Gdańsk and Riga. More specialized cruises often add Bornholm Island, Visby on the island of Gotland and Klaipéda, Lithuania. And still more specialized cruise itineraries may include the ports of the Gulf of Bothnia such as Sundsvall and Luela, Sweden along with Kemi, Vaasa and Turku, Finland as well as other lesser ports of call. The length of the itinerary and the number of ports visited is commensurate with the price for the cruise. And in some instances a cruise line will either precede or follow a Baltic Sea cruise with a Norwegian fjords itinerary thus enabling guests to book them back to back for a longer excursion.

The higher end cruise lines offer smaller ships and their staterooms are generally larger and better appointed than the mega ships belonging to the major mass market companies. There is also a higher ratio of crewmembers to passengers, thus giving more personalized and attentive service. Likewise the cuisine on the smaller up market lines is gourmet oriented, and often provides a taste of the countries being visited.

The greatest disadvantage for many in traveling on a smaller ship that carries fewer passengers is the lack of lavish entertainment because their theaters and casinos are relatively small. One must choose between having a more sedate and elegant atmosphere or "glitz" and glamour of the larger vessels.

The greatest advantage of traveling on a smaller vessel is in its ability to access ports of call the mega liners cannot visit, and even in the major ports of call, smaller ships are able in many instances to dock at facilities closer to the city centers rather than in the commercial port areas. This is a definite advantage when it comes to not having to spend valuable time riding shuttle busses to and from each city. The large mass market ships provide shuttle busses, usually at a fee for each transfer, and the hordes of people gathering to board the busses can be rather daunting.

The higher end cruise lines also have a price schedule that is more all-inclusive, resulting in there being no additional charges for alcoholic beverages, bottled water, shuttle transfers in ports and in end of cruise gratuities. One up market line even includes all tours in the fixed price of the cruise, a trend that is likely to spread.

For those who are new to cruising, here are some basic tips that will help to maximize your voyage:

* Always book an outside cabin if traveling on one of the larger ships that offer less expensive interior cabins, which have neither a window nor a veranda. Interior cabins can be quite claustrophobic because it is always necessary to use artificial

illumination. At night these cabins are totally dark to where a nightlight is needed in the event you want to get out of bed for any reason.

* To economize, book an outside cabin with a window, as these are generally on the lower passenger decks where a veranda is not provided. One advantage if the sea should become rough or even moderately choppy is that being lower down in the ship equals more stability when the ship begins to pitch or roll. And the Baltic Sea weather is generally so mild that sitting out on your own balcony is something that you in most instances will not choose to do.

* Although forward cabins are offered lower prices, be aware that the ship's maneuvering thrusters and anchors are forward. You will be exposed to a fair amount of noise when the ship is docking or leaving port, and this can often interrupt your sleep, especially if you tend to be a light sleeper.

* If having the opportunity to enjoy fresh air at any time, even if the weather is very mild or downright chilly is important to you, then it is wise to book a cabin with a veranda.

* Whenever possible book a cabin in mid ship, as when a ship begins to pitch the mid-section acts like the fulcrum in that it experiences far less movement than either forward or aft cabins. Most often the Baltic Sea is quite calm during summer, but on occasion squalls can cause the sea to become choppy. For those cruises beginning or terminating in England or The Netherlands you may experience rough seas in the waters of the North Sea or Straits of Dover. And if you are doing back-to-back cruises that include the Norwegian fjords, the waters along the Atlantic coast of Norway can become rough at any time of year.

* If you should become queasy during periods of rough weather and pitching or rolling sea, it is best to go up on deck and breath some fresh air. Also by staring off at the horizon the body surprisingly is less stressed by motion. But if you are unable to go out on deck because of the danger presented during really inclement weather, it is still possible to sit near a window and from time to time look out to sea, toward the horizon. Fear also plays a role in the way you feel during rough seas. If you become frightened that the ship may capsize or sink, it will only heighten your feeling of uneasiness. Remember that ships can take a lot of punishment, and it is almost unthinkable for a modern cruise liner to go down in rough weather.

* Starving one's self when feeling queasy will only make the condition worse. Dry crackers or toast along with hot tea is one way to calm an irritated stomach. And there are patches, pills or injections available from the ship's medical office to calm extreme discomfort.

* Be prepared for sudden changes in the weather. During summertime, the average temperatures in the Baltic Sea region are between 15 and 26 degrees Celsius or 62 and 82 degrees Fahrenheit. Occasional summer rainstorms can drop temperatures and it is easy to become chilled or soaked if not properly dressed or carrying an umbrella. Dressing in layers is the best way to accommodate the changes that can

occur on a given day. And yes there are occasional hot, humid days when the sky is blue, the sun feels strong and temperatures can climb up to 31 degrees Celsius or 90 degrees Fahrenheit, but these are the exception rather than the rule.

* Do not over indulge in eating or drinking. It is best to pace yourself and try and eat normally, as you would at home. Overindulgence only leads to discomfort and added weight gain.

* Electric voltage on board most international cruise ships there is both the 110 North American standard and the 220 European standard. But in non-international brand hotels prior to or post cruise, you will often find only the European standard. Thus for hair dryers or electric shavers and all battery chargers, you may wish to have an adapter along to expedite use of these appliances.

* When in port, weigh the option of going on organized tours against freelancing and visiting on your own. If you have any sense of adventure, a local map, public transit information and the names of basic venues make it possible to see as much, if not more, in a relaxed atmosphere in contract to being shepherded around as part of a tour group. Also by striking off on your own you have more opportunity to mingle with and meet local residents. With the exception of Russia, English has become a widely spoken second language.

 * When visiting Russia you cannot venture off on your own unless you have a visa in your passport or come from a handful of countries that do not require a visa. Without having a visa or being from a country not requiring one you are limited to being on shore only when participating in ship sponsored tours or private excursions arranged through a travel company licensed to provide the proper documentation required by the Russian authorities. Further visa information will be found later in this chapter.

* When starting a cruise, arrive at least 24 to 36 hours ahead of the departure and spend a minimum of one night in the port of embarkation. This enables you to recover from jet lag and to become acclimated to a new environment. Likewise this may be your only chance to experience the flavor of the port of embarkation which is often either Copenhagen, Stockholm, London or Amsterdam.

* When disembarking, it is also recommended that you spend at least one night in the final port of call before flying home. Two nights is preferable, as most cruises end in one of the major ports where there is a lot to see and do. Again the ports of disembarkation will be Copenhagen, Stockholm, London or Amsterdam.

* When on shore in the Baltic Sea countries, it is safe to eat without fear of gastrointestinal upset. The countries of the Baltic maintain a high degree of sanitation, and good restaurants abound. Only in Saint Petersburg, Russia is it recommended not to drink tap water because of an endemic local microbe that our bodies cannot tolerate. Elsewhere in the region, local water supplies are safe. Most restaurants, however, provide bottled water throughout the Baltic region.

* Violent crime in the Baltic Sea region is minimal. The ports of call on the itineraries of most ships are exceptionally safe. However, pickpockets are found almost everywhere that tourists will be seen in greater numbers. So wise precautions always apply regarding not keeping a wallet in a back pocket, not showing large sums of money and for women to keep a tight rein on their handbags. But you should feel totally comfortable walking even in areas that are not regularly frequented by tourists. There are very few local neighborhoods that might be considered moderately risky.

* The use of credit cards is widespread at all major restaurants and shops. However, in Europe data chips are the norm. If your credit card has a data chip, insert it into the front of the credit card machine and follow the prompts. You will either enter a pin code or wait for the receipt to be issued and then sign it. Cards without a data chip will require a special pin code. Check with your credit card service before leaving home.

* In the Baltic Sea region there are still numerous national currencies in use. And in most of the region's countries American or Canadian dollars are not readily accepted. However, in many of the countries that use their own currency, the Euro will sometimes be accepted. Most small vendors do demand their own local currency for purchases. To date, Denmark, Sweden, Russia and Poland still use their own currency, as does Norway if you happen to be adding a fjord segment to your itinerary.

* Returning to the ship is normally expedited by having your cruise identification card handy to be swiped by the security officers. Packages and large handbags are generally put through an x-ray machine similar to what is used at airports. And passengers pass through an arch to screen for any major metal objects.

* Most ships offer hand sanitizers at the gangway and recommend that you sanitize your hands upon return. This is not mandatory, but it never hurts to be cautious. The Baltic Sea region is one of the cleanest parts of the world, but still a bit of extra precaution is a good policy.

* For countries in the Western Hemisphere, visas are not necessary for any of the Baltic countries except Russia. For nations such as Argentina, Chile, Brazil, China, Hong Kong, Kazakhstan and Israel no visa is required to enter Russia. Without a visa, you will be forced to remain on board except when you hold a bona fide tour ticket issued by the cruise line or a reputable tour company authorized by the Russian government. With a visa, you have the freedom to leave the ship at any time and explore, dine or shop at your leisure. I strongly urge you to secure a Russian visa before departing home. Saint Petersburg is a vibrant city and you will find that once you are there, you will want to get off on your own, especially in the evening to enjoy a meal or just to walk during the long "white nights." But without a visa, you will essentially be held prisoner on board the ship, as you may only depart with an authorized ship's tour ticket or a prearranged tour through a reputable, licensed company. Securing a Russian visa is a somewhat complex process, but it is not that difficult. You can use the services of one of the travel service companies that secures

visa for travelers, and then the amount of work you need to do to obtain the visa is minimal. And once in Russia, it is not possible to obtain a visa. Over the years I have always had a visa for Russia. It has afforded me the opportunity to explore in ways that you cannot do even with a private tour because you will still have a car and guide. Saint Petersburg has a good transportation network of busses, trolley cars and a Metro. Yes it is daunting to use, but there are limited signs written in English to help visitors. The advantage of the visa is to give you freedom to get to know Russia and its people. And you can also explore its cuisine by having meals on shore, which is a gastronomic treat.

CURRENCY OF THE BALTIC STATES

The currency of any country is both a reflection of its national pride as well as a look at the people that have played a prominent role in its historical development. However, with the impact of the European Union, many of the countries in the Baltic have switched over to the use of the Euro, which is essentially very nondescript and does not give one a feel for the country.

At present, there are still several diverse currencies in use around the Baltic Sea. This is definitely a drawback for foreign visitors because of the need to maintain so many different currencies while traveling. In countries that use their own currency, it is next to impossible to use American or Canadian dollars for local purchases. Street vendors and small restaurants generally will not accept credit cards, and thus you will need to have local currency. If you go on tours provided by your cruise line or have private arrangements, it is customary to tip the driver/guide, and they prefer their own currency so as to not be forced to then go to a currency exchange office. However, there are currency exchange bureaus in most major ports, but their rates of exchange are not always the most favorable. It is best to purchase small amounts of the currency you will need from your own bank prior to departure. An alternative is to use a local ATM in the country where you wish to purchase their currency, as the rates are more favorable than a currency exchange bureau.

At present the following countries do not use the Euro and have no future plans to switch to a unified currency:
  Denmark uses the Danish Kroner
  Norway uses the Norwegian Kroner
  Poland uses the Złotych
  Russia uses the Ruble
  Sweden uses the Swedish Kroner

Euro banknotes used in Finland, Estonia, Latvia, Lithuania and Germany

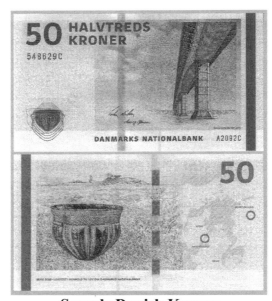

Sample Danish Kroner

Sample Swedish Kroner

Sample Russian Ruble

Sample Polish Zlotych

BALTIC SEA GEOGRAPHY

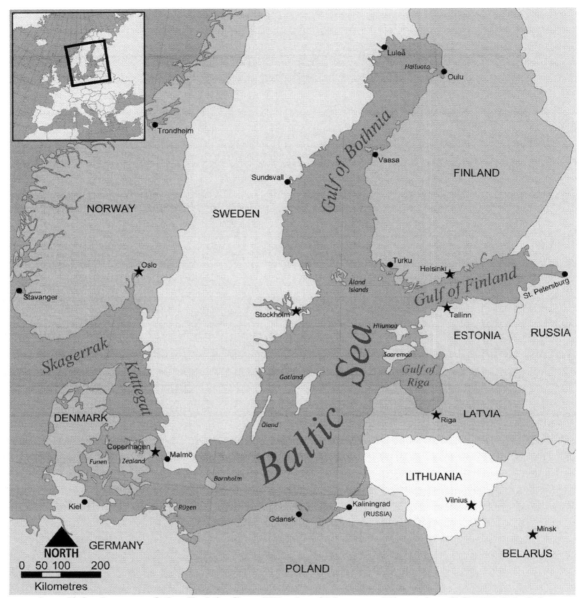

A political map of the Baltic Sea (Work of NormanEinstein, CC BY SA 3.0, Wikimedia.org)

Many people do not have an appreciation for geography as a result of the way in which it was taught, especially in North American schools. Having to memorize which mountains were the highest and which rivers were the longest was what most of us remember. I found the topic captivating even the way it was taught in grammar school. As a professional geographer, I have always believed that such rote memorization for most people takes the joy out of learning about new places, their landscapes and people. Modern geography is a discipline that examines the natural landscape as the home of mankind. It then proceeds to explore how groups of people have come to develop their culture in a given locale, how they have interacted with other people and how they have molded the natural landscape to create what we see, that being a combined physical and cultural landscape. And for anyone who travels, it is essential to have some understanding of the visual and historic aspects of the places being visited.

Essentially the Baltic Sea is a semi-enclosed arm of the northern waters of the Atlantic Ocean. To the northwest, the Scandinavian Peninsula containing Norway and Sweden separates the Baltic Sea from the open waters of the Atlantic Ocean. To the east and south lies the main body of the European continent. The Gulf of Bothnia is the northward extension of the Baltic Sea that separates the Scandinavian Peninsula from Finland. The much smaller and narrower Gulf of Finland is a second indentation stretching eastward, separating Finland from Estonia.

The link between the Baltic Sea and the Atlantic Ocean is rather complex. The Jutland Peninsula of Denmark protrudes northward off the main body of the European landmass. To the east are many moderate size islands that comprise much of Denmark, including Zealand, the home island to Copenhagen. There are narrow channels between these islands, most of them too small or shallow for large cruise ships to navigate. The major channel between the most easterly Danish islands on which the city of Copenhagen is located faces the southeastern portion of the Scandinavian Peninsula in Sweden at the city of Malmö. This deep channel is known as the Øresund, and it is the main outlet for the Baltic Sea. The Øresund widens into the Kattegat, which in turn widens into the Skagerrak that opens into the North Sea (see map below).

The Baltic Sea is approximately 1,600 kilometers or 1,000 miles long and 200 kilometers or 125 miles wide. It is not a deep body of water, its average depth being 54 meters or 180 feet with a maximum depth of just over 157 meters or 1,500 feet in a trench off the coast of Sweden. The surface area of the Baltic Sea is just over 255,545 square kilometers or 145,000 square miles, about the size of the American state of Montana. Because it is almost landlocked, the waters of the Baltic Sea are not exposed to the massive winter storms of the North Sea.

The Baltic Sea is a young body of water, its basin having been carved during the last glacial advance. As glacial ice began its retreat, melt water filled the basin and created the sea. This process occurred around 11,700 years ago. The present shape of the sea was completed around 10,000 years ago.

Given its nearly landlocked position with the only mixing occurring where the waters of the Baltic Sea mingle with the Atlantic Ocean through Denmark, the sea is not nearly as saline as the open ocean. There are so many fresh water rivers draining into the Baltic Sea from the Scandinavian Peninsula and the rest of mainland Europe, thus diluting the normal oceanic saline content. The lower salinity impacts the types of plant and animal communities that live in its waters.

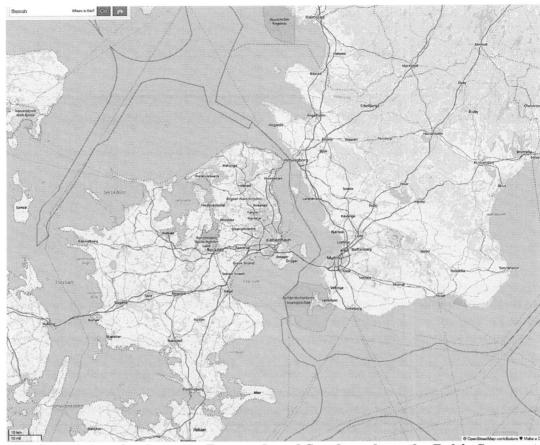

The Øresund region between Denmark and Sweden where the Baltic Sea meets the North Sea (© OpenStreetMap contributors)

SCANDINAVIAN PENINSULA: The land surrounding the Baltic Sea is generally flat to gently rolling with localized outcrops of hills. The nearest mountains are those of the Scandinavian Peninsula along the border between Norway and Sweden. They separate the river drainage between those flowing directly to the Atlantic Ocean and those flowing across Sweden to the Gulf of Bothnia. Sweden was heavily scoured by glacial ice, and this exhibits a pattern of thousands of lakes with a very complex interlocking of small rivers and streams that ultimately reach the sea. The Swedish coast is deeply indented by the sea and is lined with many thousands of rocky islands. The land is covered by a mix of thick forest composed of both broadleaf deciduous trees and conifers interspersed with farmland. Farther north the forest ultimately gives way to the bleak landscape of the tundra, but such environments are much farther north than Stockholm, and these regions are not visited by the majority of cruise ships except those few that do a circle around the Gulf of Bothnia.

On the western side of the Scandinavian Peninsula the mountainous rib was heavily glaciated with tongues of glacial ice extending westward to the Atlantic Ocean. During the great ice ages, the river channels were scoured and deepened so that after the last major glacial advance, rising sea levels flooded these channels creating the present day magnificent fjords of Norway.

THE MAINLAND LANDSCAPES: Finland is very similar to Sweden in that it contains thousands of lakes, mixed forests but only has limited farmland in its far southern margins. Most of Finland is quite flat to gently rolling and composed of hard granitic rock left over after the top layers of sediment were scraped clean by glacial ice.

The same landscape as Finland extends into Russia. There are several major lakes of glacial origin, Lake Ladoga being the largest. Saint Petersburg is built on marshes formed where the great Neva River drains from glacially created Lake Ladoga, Europe's largest body of fresh water, into the Gulf of Finland.

The southern margins of the Baltic Sea extending from Poland all the way around to Denmark are part of the North European Plain. Here the land is quite different in that the glaciers deposited fine sediments in what is now a gently rolling landscape rich in nutrients and given over primarily to farmland. There are heavier populations per square kilometer or mile in Poland, Germany and Denmark, thus little forest cover has survived over the centuries. The landscape is still very beautiful but has more of a manicured manmade appearance than in the lands along the northern shores of the Baltic Sea.

Climatically the entire Baltic Sea region experiences mild to warm summers with periods of rainfall that help nourish the land. Autumn is brilliant wherever there are broadleaf deciduous trees that bring rich pockets of gold, orange and red to the landscape. Winter in the Baltic Sea region is notoriously cold and damp. Closer to the Atlantic Ocean in Denmark and far southern Sweden the amounts of snow are far lower, but gray skies and drizzly rain typify the maritime influences. As one goes farther inland or north, the winters become far colder and snow dominates. If you remember the Hollywood movie "Doctor Zhivago," it was filmed in Finland and was supposed to represent Siberia. The scenes of a frosted landscape characterize these lands around much of the Baltic Sea. However, in the last 50 years, global warming has started to moderate the severity of the winters in the Baltic Sea region, but winter is still a long and cold season despite the ongoing moderation. At one time the Baltic Sea would freeze over and navigation would come to a standstill. Today the ice is thinner and the period of deep freeze is of shorter duration than it was half a century ago. Only on rare occasions will the sea freeze over the way it did in mid 20th century. At one time it was possible to drive a car from the Swedish coast to Finland during the winter, saving over 2,00 kilometers in the auto route between Stockholm and Helsinki.

Land's End at the top of Denmark's Jutland Peninsula

Southern Sweden's gentle countryside

The Taiga forests of Finland

The shores of Russia's Lake Ladoga – largest in Europe

Northern Polish Plains

Northern German Plain outside Hamburg

A BRIEF BALTIC SEA HISTORY

To best understand the culture and the landscape of any region visited, it is important to know something of the history of the region. It is the course of history that molds the culture, creates the visual landscape with regard to both the physical and human elements seen. Architecture, transportation networks, farming patterns and the amount of natural forest or grassland are all impacted by the succession of events that took place in the past. And for this reason history plays a major role in what the visitor encounters. This is why I place a lot of emphasis in each chapter on the history of the port of call, and of course on its parent country. You are in effect looking at layers of history and can only interpret the visual landscape through its past history. So many of the famous sites you will be visiting are vestiges of the past history of each port of call you visit.

At the time of ancient Rome, the Baltic Sea region was inhabited by a variety of tribal groups, none having formed what we would recognize as nations. Paramount among the tribes was the Norse, better known as Viking that inhabited Denmark, Norway and Sweden. They were divided into small chiefdoms each with a hereditary leader. To the south were numerous other tribal groups, the best known being the Germanic peoples. These many groups would eventually become the nations that comprise the Baltic Region of today. A mix of hunting, fishing, gathering and limited farming occupied these people, providing for their needs at what today would be recognized as a primitive level. Ultimately they accepted Christianity and began to emulate the more settled and advanced peoples living to the south of the Baltic shores.

The middle ages saw the Vikings expand outward through a combination of trade, colonization and raiding. Eventually their seed would be spread west into the British Isles and eastward deep into European Russia. The very name Russia comes from a Slavic adaptation to the name of Rurik, a Viking leader in the east, who became recognized as "Rus." And his seed led to the creation of Rossia or what in English is known as Russia. It was also the Vikings who began to call the Baltic Sea the Eastern Sea, in recognition of it being apart from the open waters of the Atlantic. Today in Germanic tongues that is how it is recognized.

By the 13th century, most Baltic Sea peoples had converted to Christianity. Numerous groups spread the Gospel, often by the sword. And with conversion came an end to the dread of Viking raids, as even these fierce warriors began to look more inward and consolidated into kingdoms, ultimately accepting Christian teachings.

Baltic Sea history from the time of the Middle Ages includes many conflicts, as trade in wood, flax, amber, furs, salt and other local products brought potential wealth. And with riches came war. During the 13th and 14th centuries, a trade federation known as the Hanseatic League dominated both the North Sea and much of the Baltic region with the Dutch in Amsterdam and Germans in Hamburg at the heart of this trade. But by the 16th century, the powers that emerged were Denmark and Sweden in the west and a united Poland-Lithuania in the east. By the start of the 18th century, Russia began to open its window on the west through Saint

Petersburg, emerging as still another major power. At the same time Prussia also consolidated its hold over much of the territory that would later become modern Germany.

From the time of Peter the Great in the early 18th century onward through the reign of Catherine the Great and later Tsars, Russia came to be the great Baltic Sea power. The Russians also pushed south into the Black Sea region to challenge the Islamic Ottoman Empire. The Crimean War of the mid 19th century saw the involvement of the British and French with a spillover of hostilities into the eastern Baltic when the French attacked Russian garrisons in Helsinki and Saint Petersburg.

The late 19th century saw the unification of Germany in 1871. And with militant Prussia at the focal hub of this new nation, the ultimate end result was Germany's role in World War I. This war ended the German Empire, and a weak German Republic could not counter the League of Nations in their creation of the Polish Corridor that split eastern Prussia from the rest of Germany. It made a relatively weak Poland a target for future aggression. Russia saw the overthrow of the Tsar, civil war and the creation of the Soviet Union between 1917 and 1922. In the 1930's, the Nazi Party gained control of Germany and built up a massive war machine that it launched against Poland in 1939, plunging Europe and ultimately many global powers into World War II.

World War II saw Germany control the Baltic Sea region except for Sweden whose neutrality the Nazi respected. The Soviet city of Leningrad (formerly and again today Saint Petersburg) managed to hold out against a German blockade for over 900 days, but Poland, the Baltic States, Denmark and Norway all fell under the boot of Nazi forces. Both in the Nazi expansion and finally retreat from the Baltic Sea, thousands of ships and planes were lost in the various engagements, essentially turning the sea floor into a military graveyard.

The modern Baltic Sea region since the fall of the Soviet Union has seen the emergence of Estonia, Latvia and Lithuania, the reunification of post-World War II Germany and most of the nations becoming members of the European Union and the North Atlantic Treaty Organization. Today trade and tourism are a major source of income for the Baltic ports in an era of peaceful coexistence unprecedented in past history.

There is a rich architecture throughout the Baltic Sea region, partly influenced by each of the historic periods and the various cultural forces that have shaped the region. Walled cities, storybook castles, magnificent cathedrals and glittering palaces have become tourist attractions. Likewise modern urban centers have developed, and they are exceptionally clean and well ordered, as a result of the high degree of cultural sophistication and prosperity of the various Baltic peoples. There is heavy industry but with careful national planning in such countries as Germany and Poland, it does not mar the landscape. Baltic cities are also important centers of commerce, banking and manufacturing.

Prehistoric burial mounds in Gamla Uppsala, Sweden

A medieval rural church in central Sweden

Ruins of an ancient Russian Orthodox monastery

Skyline of medieval Gdansk, Poland

An old northern German farmhouse

Hanseatic League architecture in Rostock, Germany

PORTS CLOCKWISE AROUND
THE BALTIC SEA

There are so many potential ports of call in the Baltic Sea that I had to consider how to organize this book. Most cruises of the Baltic Sea begin or end in Copenhagen, Denmark or Stockholm, Sweden, traveling either clockwise or counterclockwise around the shore. Thus I thought it would make more geographic sense to start with Copenhagen, which is the westernmost of the Baltic ports and then travel eastward along the northern shore, excluding the Gulf of Bothnia because it is so rare that a cruise itinerary includes this part of the sea. Then from St. Petersburg, Russia it made sense to continue along the southern shore, traveling westward toward Copenhagen. And that is how this book proceeds.

The Gulf of Bothnia is treated in a separate volume since these waters do not contain any major ports, and are seldom included in standard itineraries. It is normally the more upmarket cruise lines utilizing smaller ships that on occasion have an itinerary that includes a traverse of the Gulf of Bothnia.

Each chapter covers a single port, presenting geographic and historic background plus providing you with a guide to what to see and do. I recommend the major sights and give you opening and closing hours where necessary. The venues I offer include alternatives to the standard ship tours for those of you who want to have a greater degree of independence and an opportunity to see more than just the basics. I also offer limited restaurant recommendations because as a cruise passenger, you will only be in port during the day and for a few hours. The restaurants I recommend are ones open for lunch and serving traditional local cuisine. I also offer choice shopping recommendations, again simply because your time is limited.

Please remember that this is not an all-inclusive tour guide, as those mass-market books are aimed at people traveling on their own and needing all the minute details that cruise passengers do not require. You are living on board a floating hotel and do not need accommodation recommendations except for the two ports where most itineraries either commence or terminate, thus when in port you want the information that will maximize your visit and make it memorable.

SAINT PETERSBURG, RUSSIA

A map of the Russian Federation

VISITING RUSSIA - VISA OR NO VISA: On every major Baltic Sea itinerary the crown jewel port is Saint Petersburg, the old imperial capital of the Russian Empire. The city is rich in monumental architecture representative of the power of Tsarist Russia. But after the Communist Revolution of 1917 and the civil war that followed, the emerging Soviet Union turned its back on this grand city, relegating it to becoming an industrial giant. The old buildings deteriorated and what became Leningrad was dull and drab. But since 1991 and the emergence of the new Russia, Saint Petersburg has become the country's showplace, and today attracts millions of visitors. Many cruise lines spend up to three days docked in Saint Petersburg while some only spend two days. Either way, it is insufficient time that allows one to simply see the major highlights of this amazing city. I have been to Saint Petersburg 51 times, spending three days each visit. I still find new neighborhoods, small museums and elegant old buildings tucked away in places that are off the main tourist routes. This is a city to be savored, but at least you will be introduced to its grandeur in either a two or three-day visit.

Most visitors from North America and Western Europe do not obtain Russian visas in advance of their visit. Without a visa you are limited to leaving the ship only with a valid excursion ticket from the cruise line or from a licensed tour operator. You may be ashore only for the duration of the tour and you cannot go off on your own to explore. Contrary to what many people believe, going off on your own is as safe as in any large city of Western Europe. What is daunting for most is the lack of many English-speaking locals combined with the use of the Cyrillic alphabet, which renders reading signs next to impossible unless you have studied the language. There are a few signs written in Roman alphabet at major tourist sites and in some of the internationally recognized stores. You can easily download an alphabet with explanatory notes from the Internet and this will make it possible to at least read a street sign or the name of a store. I have taught people to be able to basically read the Cyrillic alphabet within an hour or two.

If you have a sense of adventure and are the type of person that wants to experience new things on your own without being spoon fed by a guide, I strongly urge you to go through the process and expense of obtaining a Russian visa. This enables you to come and go at will. If you are visiting on one of the large cruise ships, you will be docked in the main cruise port, which is on the outer edge of the city center. To go off on your own does require a very long walk or a ride on the local trolley bus and Metro to get to the city center. But it is not as daunting as it sounds. If you are visiting on one of the deluxe cruise lines utilizing smaller ships, you will dock along the Neva River and be within one or two kilometers from the heart of the city. It is a great advantage not only for private exploration, but even the group tours spend far less time in traffic to reach major venues.

Having the freedom of a visa enables you to sample the delectable Russian cuisine, as there are many restaurants that do not host large tour groups. The visa enables you to get out at night for dinner - a real taste treat. And yes the city is very safe to get around Saint Petersburg at night. Remember that during summer it does not get dark until almost midnight. I happen to speak and both read and write Russian, and this enables me to travel around with great ease, but there are tens of thousands of visitors who come on their own without knowing the language and they still find it a memorable experience.

There are a handful of countries that do not require a visa for a short cruise visit to Russia, and their citizens can come and go freely without the need for a tour ticket. Nationals from Argentina, Brazil, Chile, China, Hong Kong, Israel, Kazakhstan and several others are among those not needing visas.

INTERACTING WITH RUSSIANS: Russians tend to be reserve with visitors because they for the most part cannot converse with us, but if you learn just a few words of Russian it will open so many doors for you when you do venture out on your own. Russian people are so appreciative of our efforts to attempt to converse with them. And contrary to what many of us believe, they are quite welcoming in their own quiet way. Once you do make a friend in Russia, you find that they are warm, loving and very loyal. They do like those of us from the West even though our governments may not always be on the best of terms. It is always best when visiting among Russians to not talk of political matters unless you have come to know the person quite well, or in cases where they bring up the topic.

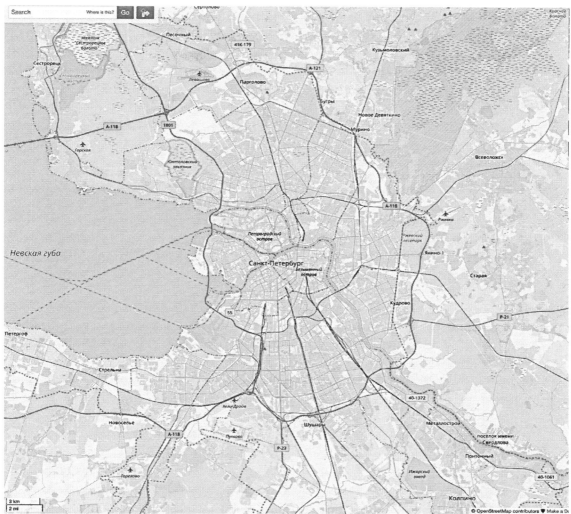

Greater Saint Petersburg written in the Cyrillic alphabet, (@OpenStreetMap.org)

THE NATURAL SETTING: Welcome to Russia. An old Tsarist saying notes that, "Russia is not a country, it's a world." Ever since the expansions brought about by Tsar Peter the Great in the early 1700's, Russia has been the world's largest nation in physical size. When in 1991 the former Soviet Union split into 15 individual nations, Russia itself still remained as the world's largest country in land area. It is hard to imagine Russia's scope. Modern Russia contains 17, 098,296 square kilometers or 6,601,670 square miles, making it nearly the size of the total United States and most of Canada combined. To imagine the magnitude of the country, picture yourself getting on a train in San Francisco and going to New York and then staying on the train while crossing the Atlantic Ocean, eventually reaching Paris, France. That gives you an idea of the east to west distance across Russia that one can travel by rail, from Moscow to Vladivostok. In actuality, the country is even wider as there are still well over 1,600 kilometers or 1,000 miles in longitude between Vladivostok and the far eastern edge of Siberia, where Russia meets Alaska. Yes Alaska, because Russia is America's neighbor as hard as that may be to believe. American readers may remember that vice presidential candidate Sarah Palin in 2000 said, "I can see Russia from my front porch." She as an Alaskan meant that

in a figurative manner, as Alaska is a neighbor to Russia. There are two islands in the Bering Straits that are less than three kilometers or two miles apart. One belongs to the United States and the other to Russia. During the Cold War years, soldiers stationed on these two islands would supposedly exchange visits during long, dark winter nights, crossing over the frozen waters via snowmobile, sharing beer, vodka and cards, of course in secret. Whether this is true or not, neither military will confirm.

In May 2015, I was visiting Petropavlovsk on the Kamchatka Peninsula in far eastern Siberia as part of a Trans Pacific cruise. I was being escorted around by the ship's local tour representative and when we were having lunch, I asked, "If there were roads connecting Petropavlovsk with Saint Petersburg, approximately how long a journey would it be?" He thought for a moment and then answered, "If there were roads, which there are not, it would be approximately 16,000 kilometers (10,000 miles) between the two cities." This example should further impress you with the immensity of Russia as the world's largest nation. Yet its population is only144,500,000, less than half that of the United States.

Only a miniscule piece of this great nation fronts on the Baltic Sea, but it contains a city that has embodied the grand era of the Tsars as its window to the west. The city of St. Petersburg is located in the western end of the country, actually along a narrow strip of coastline on the Gulf of Finland. With loss of former territory, the city is only about 112 kilometers or 70 miles from the Estonian border to the southwest and 90 miles northwest to the Finnish border. The city occupies what was once swampy ground along the banks of the Neva River where it enters the Gulf of Finland. Behind the city, about 46 kilometers or 30 miles distance is the massive Lake Ladoga, the largest lake in Europe. Lake Ladoga is the result of glacial scour during the last ice age and it is a major body of water covering 17,611 square kilometers or 6,800 square miles. The Neva River empties from this massive lake into the Gulf of Finland, carrying a tremendous volume of water right through Saint Petersburg.

The entire area around Saint Petersburg is thickly forested in spruce, larch and birch, what is referred to as taiga, that great boreal forest that stretches across Eurasia and North America. There are hundreds of small lakes and ponds dotting the region, and it is essentially quite beautiful in a panoramic manner rather than a spectacular one. It is a shame that few cruise visitors ever arrange for tours out into the countryside because there is so much to see in the city. And the cruise lines concentrate their efforts on offering excursions to the most important of the cultural and historic sites. Only those cruise lines that offer a one-day sightseeing excursion by fast train to Moscow provide an opportunity to see the countryside of northwestern Russia, but only in passing while journeying to and from the national capital.

Saint Petersburg has very long and cold winters with a minimum of daylight hours. Temperatures can drop well below freezing for weeks on end. Summer may be a short season, but days can warm up to where one does not need a jacket. And the most beautiful part of summer is what Russians call the "White Nights." From the middle of June to late July there are over 21 hours of daylight, and the evening light casts a golden hue across the city. It is on such golden evenings that many shipboard guests wish they had a visa so as to be able to take a walk and enjoy such evenings.

RUSSIA'S DYNAMIC HISTORY: A visit to Saint Petersburg is all about history. No other city encompasses its history into the venues that visitors come to see in the same way as does Saint Petersburg. To understand the nature of the city of St. Petersburg, it is first necessary to know something about Russian history. Consider this section of the chapter essential to developing an appreciation for the sights you will see when visiting.

The city was born out of the desire of one Tsar to change the face of Russia, which he certainly did. Brutal would be an understatement for the whole of Russian history. Russians have known not only a harsh and unforgiving environment that has limited the country's ability to adequately provide for its raw material needs, but also their history has been one of bloodshed, depravities committed by the Tsars and wars fought both internally and externally. And from 1918 until 1991, the country was ruled over by the Communist ideology that opposed individualism and material wealth. It is often stated that the reason why there appears to be a somber quality to the people stems from the hardships that have been endured by the masses over many centuries. This may be an over simplification, but it is food for thought. The other factor you must accept is that in traditional Russian culture it is actually considered to be impolite to smile at strangers you do not know, so this gives the illusion that Russians are unfriendly.

It was during the ninth century that Slavonic tribes began to settle in the Ukraine, Belarus and in the Valdai Hills around what is now Moscow. Previously, Scythians inhabited the land, dating back to the third century BC, later having been overrun by the Germanic Goths, ancient enemies of Rome. The Slavonic people are believed to have originated in the rugged mountains of the Balkans, slowly migrating out onto the Steppes of the Ukraine. The first actual Russian state does not occur until around 850, its name being the Grand Principality of Rus, the name taken from the ancient Viking colonial leader Rurik who established settlements in the area between present day Moscow and Kiev. When the Principality collapsed in 1132, central Russia was divided into small city-states that often warred with one another. In the middle of the 13th century, much of Russia fell under the domination of the Mongol hordes. By 1462, the Grand Principality of Muscovy emerged, given its commanding position over the headwaters of the Volga River. The first leader of the Principality to forcibly unite all of the various fiefdoms into one large nation was Ivan IV, known as Ivan the Terrible, who proclaimed himself Tsar of all the Russias. The term Tsar was taken from Caesar, a reference to the grand rulers of ancient Rome. From 1533 to 1584, he consolidated his power in a brutal reign that was filled with murders and intrigues. During a rage, the Tsar clubbed his own son and heir to death, just one example of what occurred during his time on the throne.

Following the death of Ivan, Russia was plunged into a series of court intrigues, a Polish invasion and finally it emerged still unified under the first of the Romanoff Tsars, Mikhail in 1613. But it was under the reign of Mikhail's grandson, Peter I, ultimately known as Peter the Great, that Russia became a world power. Tsar Peter ruled from 1696 to 1725. During his reign, he decreed that the Boyars or court nobles must wear more western style dress, shave off their beards and become more accustomed to the ways of the outside world.

Once Tsar Peter had solidified his hold on the throne, the Tsar set off on a journey of several years, visiting the Netherlands to learn about shipbuilding and trade, and then to England and France where he saw grand and elegant lifestyles while discovering the latest trends in the sciences. He came to realize just how backward and isolated his country was. And he knew that Russia had to be opened up to the ideas and customs of the West if it was to ever take its place as a modern European nation. But how to achieve this was the question that Tsar Peter had to ponder.

Upon returning to Russia, Tsar Peter decided that the capital must be moved from its inland location in Moscow to a window on the Gulf of Finland from which it would be possible to travel by sea to the western nations of Europe, at least during the summer months. Peter pressed into service thousands of craftsmen to drain the swampy ground and began erecting a new capital, but one whose architecture would be patterned after that of Paris. And thus began the development of the city of Saint Petersburg. The Tsar forced the nobility to move to the new city, and he commanded them to build palatial homes. At the same time that he was developing his new city, he also oversaw the expansion of his empire into the reaches of Siberia and down into the steppe and desert lands of Central Asia.

The city of Saint Petersburg got its greatest boost in terms of architectural construction and grandeur under the Empress Catherine, known as Catherine the Great. Apart from Peter, she became the most famous of all Russian rulers, and she was not even Russian. She was born a German princess in a rather obscure backwater principality, but she was sent to Russia to marry the nephew and heir of the Empress Elizabeth, daughter of Peter the Great. Catherine was baptized into the Orthodox Church and quickly learned the court intrigues in the palace. Her husband was not a willing partner, and to this day it is unclear if the son she bore was truly his. After her husband came to the throne upon the death of Elizabeth, in 1762, a palace coup deposed her feeble husband, and with the support of the military, she was proclaimed Empress of Russia, not just the regent for her son Paul. She ruled in autocratic fashion until her death in 1796. She was responsible for many cultural reforms, the development of the arts and she expanded the empire to the Black Sea and deep into Siberia.

But Catherine's greatest accomplishments were in Saint Petersburg. She expanded the Winter Palace into its present state of glory, adding a great art collection, which is today second only to the Louvre in Paris. She also expanded what was a small summer palace south of the city into one of the world's most splendid palaces – Tsarskoye Selo. Catherine brought a grand European elegance to the city, and this curried great favor among the nobility. However, her palace love affairs with military officers and politicians meant that nobody in government was on solid ground. By the time of her death, Saint Petersburg was considered to be one of the glittering capitals of Europe. But of course all this grandeur was at the expense of the poor peasants whose labors built the fabulous palaces and churches that made the city grand. Russia at the time of Catherine was a nation of two classes. There was the nobility and its retainers along with wealthy merchants. These people, a minority of the total population, lived in luxury. Many actually lived lives of splendor, surrounded by the most elegant of furnishings and dressed in the utmost of high fashion clothing. Then there were the masses, or peasants. The majority lived on the land, but not as independent farmers. Most were consigned as serfs to the landed estates of the nobility, essentially one step above slave labor. In the cities, the urban poor were those who tended to the most menial of jobs or worked in the small factories and craft shops.

Following Catherine's death, the next succession of Tsars varied from totally autocratic to somewhat benevolent. In 1812, the forces of Tsar Alexander I combined with an unusually brutal winter defeated Napoleon, ending the greatest threat of its day to the Russian Empire. In 1861, Tsar Alexander II freed millions of peasant serfs from their indentured service to the landed nobility. This ultimately led to his assassination and to a terribly autocratic rule by his son, Tsar Alexander III. His rule was the first of many underlying factors that would lead to the eventual downfall of the House of Romanoff.

Tsar Nicholas II and his beautiful wife Tsarina Alexandra were to be the last of the Romanoff line and the end of an era for Russia. His uncle, King Edward VII of the United Kingdom, had warned him that he needed to establish a parliamentary system of government and end autocratic rule. The Tsar tried the concept, but when the Duma (parliament) appeared to show a degree of independence, he closed it down. The Tsar embroiled Russia in a war with Japan that American President Theodore Roosevelt had to negotiate a peace treaty to conclude in 1905, and this made the Tsar quite unpopular. It also angered Japan's leaders because it kept them from what would have been a victory over Russia in far eastern Siberia.

There was the issue regarding the young heir who suffered from hemophilia. A Siberian monk by the name of Rasputin was able to convince the Tsarina that he had mystical powers to heal. At times Rasputin appeared to be able to help the young Tsarevich, but in so doing, he wheedled his way into the inner circle, and there were fears among the nobility that he had a profound influence upon both the Tsar and the Tsarina. It was decided among a group of nobles that Rasputin had to die. He was invited one night to the Usupov Palace, served poisoned sweets and wine, which he survived. He was later shot and finally thrown into the one of the canals of the Neva River. Ultimately, he died, and nobody was ever apprehended for the crime.

In 1914, Russia entered the war against Germany and the Austro-Hungarian Empire because of their longstanding pledge to defend Serbia. The war was a disaster and the Tsar was unable to muster sufficient loyalty to keep troops from deserting the front. In February 1917, he was forced to abdicate, and a provisional government was established. A Bolshevik leader named Vladimir Ilich Ulyanov, later to call himself Vladimir Lenin, inspired riots in Saint Petersburg and Moscow. In October 1917, the Bolshevik forces stormed the Winter Palace and the provisional government collapsed. The Tsar and his family were exiled to Siberia, and in 1918, they were all grouped together for what was supposedly an official photograph before being moved to another location. But they were brutally executed by firing squad and their bodies were then soaked in acid, burned and buried. Thus the Communists felt assured that there would be no turning back.

The bodies of the Tsar and his family were discovered in the early 1990's, identified through DNA, matching them to Prince Phillip of the United Kingdom because of their bloodline connection through the Danish royal house. They were then returned to Saint Petersburg and given a formal state burial in the Peter and Paul Cathedral, as was befitting a Tsar, thus bringing full circle the history of tsarist Russia.

Lenin's victory was followed by years of bloody civil war, which ended in 1922 with the creation of the Union of Soviet Socialists Republics. The capital was moved back to the Kremlin in Moscow, leaving Saint Petersburg as a second-class city. Lenin thought that Saint Petersburg expressed the height of decadence and as the leader of a Communist state, the capital needed to be located in the nation's heartland. When Vladimir Lenin died in 1924, the city of Saint Petersburg was renamed Leningrad in his honor, and that name lasted until 1991. And the city became a major industrial center, leaving the grand palaces and churches to deteriorate, as they were inconsequential to Communist doctrine.

This dictatorial and monolithic state would last until the end of 1990. The Soviet Union became a powerful state, but at the expense of its people. Freedoms were highly limited, especially after Lenin died in 1924 and Joseph Stalin came to power. It is now known that his various purges and incarcerations in the notorious gulags of Siberia cost the lives of over 20,000,000 Russians. Only during World War II, when Nazi Germany invaded Russia, did Stalin find that there was true support among the masses. He did engender a certain fatherly image that the Russians seemed to need to aid in their victory over the Germans. Russia did receive massive foreign aid from the United States and the United Kingdom. Red Army determination once again combined with a brutal winter helped to defeat Germany and ultimately turn the tide of the war, but at a cost of another 20,000,000 lives.

During the war, the Nazi forces attempted to take the city of Leningrad, but were held at bay by a tenacious people and detachments of the Red Army. The Germans surrounded the city and for 900 days they attempted to starve it into submission. The city was bombarded and shelled on a regular basis and people died of not only explosions, but also of starvation and cold. Only during winter could the Red Army supply the city by driving convoys of trucks over the frozen Lake Ladoga to the east, a perilous journey both because of the dangers of thin ice toward late winter and the harassment by Nazi forces that led to several major battles along the southern margins of the lake. This was one of the most terrible of sieges in modern history. There are many monuments in Saint Petersburg to commemorate this terrible event and Russia's victories over the German forces. However, most group tours never include these monuments because the tour operators focus primarily upon the glories of Tsarist Russia before 1917. But if the Siege of Leningrad is of significant interest, you can have the ship's shore concierge staff arrange private excursions for you that will focus on this theme.

The Soviet Union became the Cold War enemy of the United States and Western Europe, especially after it too developed nuclear weapons during the 1950's. Several dictatorial leaders ruled after Stalin's death in 1953, the two most famous being Nikita Khrushchev and Leonid Brezhnev. During the 1980's, a new and moderate leader came to power. His name of course was Mikhail Gorbachev, the man who began to open the doors through his policies of glasnost and perestroika, openness and restructuring. But it was too late to restructure the system, as the Soviet Union was over extended and starting to crumble. The end came on December 31, 1990, when Mr. Gorbachev dissolved the Union of Soviet Socialist Republics. The Russian Federation emerged, and it has had its problems, scandals and is only now becoming far more stable economically.

The people of Russia have known bitter hardship throughout their long history. Yes there are many glories, and Saint Petersburg displays the opulence and elegance of a romantic era of tsarist life. But for the average Russian, just earning enough to survive has always been the primary goal. It is true that Russians love to sing and dance, and there is an exuberance to their style of folk dancing that pierces the soul. But these expressions were reserved for weddings and special occasions. Most of the music that one hears is melancholy and tugs at the heartstrings. It is a deep and moving part of the Russian soul.

In 1991, as Russia emerged out of the former Soviet Union, it quickly set about to restore old place names, bring back the role of the Orthodox Church and restore many of its monuments to the past. One of the most memorable of events was the final internment of the remains of Tsar Nicholas II and his family, brutally murdered by the Bolsheviks. Even the President of Russia attended the ceremony, marking a reestablishment of ties between the new Russia and its illustrious, if not sometimes brutal, past history. Today Saint Petersburg is the showplace of how Russia adapted itself to western ways. Its elegant palaces and churches again glitter with the aura of the old empire.

Once again people enjoy taking a stroll along Nevsky Prospekt, the grand main boulevard of the city. Looking at the glorious architecture, it is not hard to imagine being back in the days of the Tsar when this street was the place to be seen among the city's royal and noble classes. There are still many cafes that serve light meals or evening refreshments. And during the summer when the sun only dips below the horizon for a couple of hours, the buildings take on a distinct golden glow, which the Russians also refer to as the "White Nights." But in today's reality, Nevsky Prospekt is no longer just a street that caters to the rich nobility and royalty of Russia, as it once did.

THE PRESENT POLITICAL REALITY: To fully understand the nature of life in Russia when you visit Saint Petersburg, it is essential to understand the current state of foreign relations between Russia and the West. This is a sensitive topic, yet it is bound to come up during one of the excursions sponsored by the cruise line or during a private tour or when meeting Russians if you explore on your own. The vast majority of the people of Russia support the foreign doctrines of their current government led by President Vladimir Putin. In the West he has become somewhat vilified and compared to the former hard line Soviet leaders of the past. In Russia, he has a strong measure of public support, but there are those who quietly are critical of his policies. The Putin government does not readily tolerate much open criticism or hostility. The opposition has grown in recent years, but it is still very small compared to the support the president has from the majority of Russians. But being in the minority, most people are often reluctant to speak about their president, however, you will find those who do speak quite openly and reflect some of the attitudes expressed by western media. To best understand the current government, it is important to recognize the following facts:

* Government in Russia is somewhat autocratic, but this is written into the national constitution. The bulk of real power is not vested in the Duma (parliament) but rather rests with the office of the president.

* The president may serve for two consecutive six-year terms, and following an absence of one term, he may serve again for a maximum of two more consecutive terms. This leads to the potential for a strong man leader to emerge, one who can hold he reins of power for a lengthy period. President Putin has served for eight years under the old four-year term, then served as the prime minister for one term and is now back in the second six-year term of office. Some critics claim he will attempt to change the constitution to enable him to serve a third consecutive six-year term. That remains to be seen and there is little point in speculating at this time.

* The main political party that has been in power since 1991, the United Russia party holds 341 seats out of the 450 seats in the Duma. And President Putin is the party leader. This vast majority means that the Duma is fully supportive of the President's decisions.

* The United Russia party has been quite forceful in suppressing outward opposition to its policies. Many westerners believe that the President and key party officials have used intimidation and bribery to achieve an ongoing role as the preeminent force in the country

* President Putin has appealed to national pride by exerting pressure on western leaders to recognize Russia as a major political player in world affairs. His outward actions have unfortunately brought western condemnation of many political actions, sanctions against the economic sector and in the end has entrenched the Russian leadership into an adversarial relationship with the West.

Misunderstanding of Russian political processes and the sentiment of a vast segment of the populace created this current atmosphere of confrontation with Russian leaders becoming more intransigent in flexing their political and military muscle. This has become quite evident in the recent campaign of Russian military actions in support of the Syrian president contrary to the position of the majority of western leaders.

When Russia took control of the Crimean Peninsula in 2014, western leaders and media condemned the action without any attempt to understand the underlying factors involved. This immediately started a rapid deterioration in relations between Russia and the West. Yes it was an aggressive act on Russia's part, and it was a total contravention of international relations. But President Putin, with a vast majority of Russians behind him, saw it differently. From their collective point of view, Crimea had been a part of Russia since Tsarist times when it was taken away from the Ottoman Empire. The population of the peninsula was and had always been predominantly Russian. During the 1950's, Soviet leader Nikita Khrushchev transferred the territory to the Ukrainian Soviet Socialist Republic to quell their insistence that they needed more coastal access. It was an inconsequential matter because Ukraine was a part of the Soviet Union. The population of Crimea was still Russian and Moscow still controlled the whole of the nation.

When the Soviet Union dissolved in 1991, the Ukraine leaders chose independence, and Crimea thus was lost to Russia since it had been acknowledged as part of the Ukraine. A treaty was signed enabling the large Russian naval base in Sevastopol to be leased, and therefore the Russian military maintained a strong position in the region and contributed heavily to the economic base.

In 2012 when the Ukrainian people began to pressure their government for closer economic and social ties with the European Union, the Ukrainian leader who was very closely allied to Russia's President Putin, resisted. This ultimately led to massive protests that became somewhat violent and led to the president fleeing the country. Elections were held and a very pro-western president was elected. This in turn angered the Russian minority in Crimea and also in the industrialized eastern portion of Ukraine where there have been close economic and trade links with Russia dating back to the Soviet Era.

Russian leadership saw an opportunity to win back the Crimean Peninsula and this helped stir up feelings that led to a 2014 referendum in which over 90 percent of the populace voted for a reunification with Russia. And the Russian military presence made it impossible for the government of the Ukraine to counter the momentum that swept the region. Thus Crimea was officially annexed by Russia, a move that was not in accordance with international law because of the rapidity in which it occurred, especially without any concurrence by the Ukrainian government. Although Russia had sufficient grounds to make a case before the United Nations, they chose immediate military action and this has cost them dearly with regard to relations with the West.

The events of Crimea stimulated rebellion among those of Russian cultural origin and those sympathetic to maintaining ties with Russia in the eastern Ukraine. And ultimately this has led to what is essentially a civil war in that part of the country. And clearly there has been Russian assistance to the rebel forces, a matter that has further angered western leaders. At the moment in early 2019, the situation is essentially a stalemate.

It is within the context of the events herein described that visitors are still cruising to Saint Petersburg. I felt it important to help clarify what underlies the current tensions between Russia and the West. But as a scholar of Russian history and as a traveler who has been traveling and cruising to Russia numerous times each summer since 2010 while presenting my lectures on board ship, I can offer full assurance that you will be safe when visiting Russia. Tourism is a major source of income to the country, especially to Saint Petersburg. Russian people on a non-governmental level do not hold it against the West that our governments and theirs are not in agreement over the issues of Ukraine, ISIS and the Middle East in general. But despite these political divisions, we are welcomed and respected. I do caution you to be circumspect in the way in which you answer any questions of a political nature. Remember that you are a guest in their country. Russians are essentially proud of their nation and its present accomplishments and they do not want to be "lectured to" or spoken down to by westerners. The Soviet Era is over, and they do not want us to cast them in that light. Likewise, we are treated overall with respect so long as we show a mutual level of respect despite whatever feelings to the contrary any of us may have. You are in Saint Petersburg to view the historical marvels of its past glory, so enjoy it.

THE PHYSICAL LAYOUT OF THE CITY OF SAINT PETERSBURG: Saint Petersburg occupies very low-lying ground along both shores of the Neva River along with several large islands within the river's massive delta (see maps at the end of the chapter). The Neva is a short, but wide river that empties from Lake Ladoga 46 kilometers or 30 miles to the east of the city into the Gulf of Finland, the easternmost arm of the Baltic Sea.

With the potential for storm surges brought on by passing weather systems now combined with rising sea levels, a massive dike has been built across the Gulf of Finland connecting the southern shore with the northern and carrying atop it an expressway that links Kronstadt Island with the mainland. The island has been and continues to be Russia's naval base for the Baltic and North Atlantic fleet. To enable ships to enter and leave Saint Petersburg, there is a large opening in the dike that can be closed by two great gates. The expressway is carried under the opening in a deepwater tunnel. This is a very impressive project and Kronstadt is a fascinating place to visit now that it is open to the public for the first time since the Bolshevik Revolution of 1917.

When the city was founded, it was necessary to dig canals to help drain the land so that building foundations could be stabilized in the soft alluvial soil. Today these canals serve primarily as routes for small pleasure and tourist boats to navigate among some of the oldest of the city's neighborhoods. Beyond the river delta and its low-lying bottom land the countryside rises slightly into a gently rolling landscape, but there are few hills and no mountains anywhere in sight. The countryside is covered in coniferous taiga forest interspersed with groves of birch trees. And there are numerous small lakes and ponds, many of them today being surrounded by dachas (country homes) for weekend use. There is only a small amount of agriculture around Saint Petersburg because of the length and severity of the winter. Dairy cattle, root vegetables, apple orchards and some rye, barley and oats can be raised in the local area.

The heart of the city occupies the land south of the main branch of the river known as the Bolshaya Neva. Suburbs extend well to the south where the land begins to rise up out of the bottomland. The two largest islands, Vasilevsky and Petrogradsky, are both heavily urbanized and each one houses several hundred thousand residents. The smaller northern islands of the delta provide recreational space for sports venues along with large dachas for the wealthy on Krestovsky Island.

The north shore of the Neva's northern branch is known as the Primorsky District. It is one of the new and expanding areas of the city. Both here in Primorsky and in the suburbs south of the old central city, massive high-rise apartment complexes have developed. In these outer regions the building crane is often said to be the most common bird. There are cranes everywhere, as new apartment buildings rise. They vary in quality from large blocks housing thousands of working-class residents to narrower, elegant blocks that can cost the equivalent of many hundreds of thousands of Euro.

East of the Neva River after it bends into a north to south axis, the area has seen far less development. This area, known as the Nevsky District, has the potential for great urban growth because it is close to the city center, but it has been more industrialized in past decades and is only now starting to see more residential and commercial growth.

Fortunately for Russia, the Germans were never able to destroy Saint Petersburg during World War II, despite their great siege of the city. They cut off the city by forming a blockade across the land between the Gulf of Finland and Lake Ladoga. During winter, the Red Army was able to bring in limited supplies by truck convoys across the frozen lake and then down a well-protected road that became known as "Doroga Zhizny," meaning the Road of Life. There were many battles fought in the marshes and lowlands across this zone, but ultimately the Soviet forces prevailed. But during that siege there was tremendous loss of life.

Many of the city's landmarks and especially the two summer palaces south of the city were destroyed, but lovingly rebuilt after the war. Even under Communist rule, there was a strong appreciation for the classical and elegant architecture, thus the building of modern structures was forbidden in the city center even though initially many old buildings were allowed to languish. As Communism was replaced by free enterprise, and as Russians began to value the importance of tourism, the heart of Saint Petersburg became an attraction that could become a major selling point for visitors. And it has worked. This is a must see city for people visiting the Baltic Sea region. In fact, it is the highlight of the region. In 1990, the historic heart of Saint Petersburg and many of the outlying palaces became a UNESCO World Heritage Site, assuring the protection of the integrity of this incredible city.

New construction is relegated the second and third rings of development surrounding the old city. The second ring consists of buildings from the Communist Era – mostly gray blocks of apartments and massive government buildings. But those built in the Stalin Era are considered to have architectural merit. Many have been renovated and restored while their exteriors remain in the Stalinist style. These buildings are also valued for residential use because of the apartments having larger rooms and high ceilings. But in many parts of the middle or second ring of the city are thousands of buildings built in Khrushchev and Brezhnev Eras. These are rather unadorned blocks, many of the having been hastily built with inferior materials. Today, most of these buildings are eyesores and they are hard to modernize and make attractive. But as the city continues to grow, contractors find it more advantageous to tear them down in favor of modern 21st century high-rise housing.

In the third ring one finds the glitzy new high-rise condos and apartments that are highly sought after by Russia's new middle and upper classes. And with the newly found prosperity that has come to Russia, there are magnificent apartment blocks and condos in the city's outer ring that would resemble the finest of such buildings found in North American cities, but of course these are for the wealthy class.

Some of the new apartment blocks being built in the outer suburban areas, especially in the southwest of the city, are massive. Many are up to 30 stories in height and stretch for several blocks in length as one contiguous building. These blocks are definitely impressive and they do reflect the demand for new housing. The suburban landscape should be seen by cruise passengers other than just in passing while traveling to either Peterhoff or Catherine's Palace. They represent the progress being made in modern Russia and these suburbs are very impressive.

Several major boulevards sweep inward to the old city center, in some ways like the spokes of a wheel. Two of the most notable are Kammennostrovsky Prospekt in the north, crossing Petrogradsky Island en route to the Field of Mars. In the south, Moskovsky Prospekt is another major urban boulevard. Both are lined with older apartment blocks mixed with new construction.

What is most impressive is the development of the city's expressway system. There is one outer ring expressway that begins in Petrogradsky District and encircles the city, coming into the far southern portion of the city along the edge of the Kirovsky and Krasnoselsky Districts. The Western High Speed Diameter is a new partly elevated expressway that runs south in the northwestern part of the city, feeding in from the Finnish border. This amazing piece of construction crosses the three branches of the Neva River in its massive delta and then traverses above the major commercial docks before it joins the A118 belt expressway in the far southwest near the international airport. This route, which opened in late 2016, cuts off over one hour of travel time for people living in Petrogradsky or on Vasilevsky Island when en route to the airport or the southern suburbs.

GETTING AROUND SAINT PETERSBURG IF ON YOUR OWN: Without question, Saint Petersburg will be the highlight of any Baltic Sea cruise. No other city in the region is as large or offers as many palaces, churches and museums to the visitor. Remember that this was the capital of the entire Russian Empire for just over 200 years, especially at the peak of the era of grandeur that Russia copied from the western courts. Although visitors come to see the historic architecture from Tsarist times, modern St. Petersburg will surprise visitors with its massive high-rise construction, large shopping malls and well-designed urban parks. Saint Petersburg is presently the third largest city in Europe with a population of over 6,000,000. It is only exceeded by Moscow and London in population.

Most ship passengers will be visiting Saint Petersburg on organized excursions operated by the cruise line rather than going exploring on their own. The reason for this, as noted previously, is based upon the strictness of the Russian immigration laws. Only passengers who have secured a visa are allowed off the ship at will. There are several private tour operators that provide excursions either in groups or privately, and they will arrange the necessary documents to enable visitors to leave the ship. But just like the cruise-organized tours, visitors are only allowed off the ship for the duration of the private or small group tour. The company that I trust exclusively is Baltic Travel for all my private car and driver arrangements. You can contact them via e-mail at *welcome@baltic.spb.ru* for details and prices. Another option is to have the cruise line arrange private cars and driver/guides, but once again visitors are only allowed out for the duration of the tour. The private car option through the cruise lines, however, is very expensive.

For those who have a visa, getting around the city is difficult on one's own unless having a working knowledge of the language. Few signs outside of the tourist areas are written in English, and few people in service positions speak any language but Russian. Thus I will try to help in this section for anyone who wants to be a bit adventurous and try it on your own. The best way to explore on one's own is to hire a guide either with an automobile or one who will escort you via public transportation. And here I again highly recommend Baltic Travel. I am in no way soliciting business for them, but as a travel author and professional geographer I have come to rely upon their services exclusively.

The Metro with its elegant and ornate stations is a fast and efficient way to get around the city. However, it does not have any line that encircles the city, thus if going in a particular direction to visit a venue, one then must retrace steps back into the city center and then change to another line to head in a different direction. There are many trolley busses and regular busses that run every few minutes. But once again it is essential to know the language or have a guide, otherwise getting around will be somewhat difficult, but not impossible.

If you are traveling on board one of the large mega cruise ships it will dock at the major cruise terminal, which is located at the far end of Vasilevsky Island, requiring utilizing public transportation to reach the city center. Ship shuttle busses are not provided because so few guests have visas where they can take advantage of the opportunity to get around on their own. There is a public shuttle bus number 158 that runs every 30 minutes from Terminal Three to the Primorskaya Metro Station. From there you can take the Metro to Gostini Dvor in the heart of Nevsky Prospekt.

The cost for the shuttle is 25 Rubles and for the Metro it is 28 Rubles, and you must have Russian currency since no exchange service is possible outside of the terminal.

If you are cruising with Silversea, Regent or Seaborne, you will be docking along the Bolshaya Neva River in the city center or across the river on Vasilevsky Island. From either location you can walk to many good restaurants. Do not rely upon taxis because they often do not frequent these riverside quays, or if they do, most drivers are not versed in English. Likewise you may easily be overcharged since no meters are generally used. From the English Embankment on the city center side of the river, walk to the corner of Ploshchad Truda, cross over and then walk two blocks south to Konnogvardeysky Boulevard, which has a green strip down the middle. Walk east two blocks to the bus stop for trolley bus number 22. This bus will take you to Nevsky Prospekt for a cost of 25 Rubles. It saves you a walk of around 1.5 miles. If your ship is docked across the river on Vasilevsky Island, you simply need to walk out to the Lieutenant Schmidt Embankment, walk to the traffic light, cross over and then walk one very long block north to Bolshoi Prospekt where you will find a trolley bus stop number ten or 11. This bus will also take you to Nevsky Prospekt.

MAJOR LANDMARKS OF SAINT PETERSBURG: Most visitors coming by cruise ship will see many of the highlights of Saint Petersburg by means of being part of a variety of ship sponsored coach tours. Despite the variety of tours, they all share one element in common - conformity. You are part of a selected itinerary that gives you essentially no choice but to follow your guide and be lectured to about whatever it is you are seeing. For those willing to spend a bit more money, there is a better way to explore Saint Petersburg, one that gives you more freedom and flexibility. This is the private tour where you have a car or van with a driver and a licensed guide. I do, however, offer this warning; if you just select from various venues to visit, but without specifying your tastes or preferences, you will receive the same prepared guided lecture in each venue that you would receive on a group tour. The advantage that most people do not take is to customize what you want to see. With a car, driver and guide, you are NOT limited to the major venues that the group tours are visiting. You can explore neighborhoods, see how people live, work and shop. You can visit lesser known churches, palaces, museums or go out simply shopping. You can dine in local restaurants. You can take a tour into the countryside. You can visit a school, ride on the Metro, go to a sporting event or a folk performance. Essentially it is your choice as to what to see or do. Many tour operators will discourage such individualized activity because their guides are pre-programed to simply mirror the group tours. There are times you must simply insist that you want to do something not on the normal list of activities. There are no laws preventing you from seeing more of Russia. Over the years, I have been places and seen things that no tourist has probably ever experienced. True I always have a visa, but in the case of using a private car, that is irrelevant.

In my list of sight to see, I will be including many lesser known attractions or venues that most visitors are not even aware of. This is for the purpose of alerting you to what is available if you choose the private car option. Street addresses are not provided, as these major landmarks are so recognized visually and are identified on city maps to the point that an address would have no literal reference. I cannot possibly list every site in the city, as the majority of you who read this book are only be able to visit on guided tours without a visa or a passport from a country not in need of one. And even if you have the freedom to explore on your own, there is no way in two or three days that you will even be able to see all that I do note in this book. I have tried to make this list as broad and comprehensive as possible, broken down into major sight, lesser venues and those located outside of the city such as the summer palaces.

MY MAJOR RECOMMENDATIONS IN THE CITY (The double asterisk is denoting monuments or venues within or a part of the site denoted by a single asterisk. The listing is alphabetical by major venue):

* Alexander Nevsky Monastery - Located at the far end of Nevsky Prospekt from Palace Square, this important shrine with its adjacent cemetery that holds many famous people is also an active church, but visitors are welcome on the grounds and inside the sanctuary. However, it is necessary to first purchase a ticket. It is open daily between 6 AM and 8 PM.

* Church of the Savior on Blood (better known as the Church of the Spilled Blood) was built to memorialize Tsar Alexander II, who was assassinated in 1881. Tsar Alexander III, who ordered the church, wanted it to make a statement that would speak to the true Russia. Thus the building is more characteristic of the famous Saint Basil's Cathedral, which stands just outside of the Kremlin walls in Moscow. It has become the most iconic landmark in the city because of its true Russian flavor. During summer the church is open from 10:30 AM until 10:30 PM through the end of September. The church is closed on Wednesday. Tickets must be purchased prior to entry.

* Lady of Kazan Cathedral - This is another major working church in which services are held throughout the day. Located on Nevsky Prospekt, this massive cathedral has a Romanesque exterior, but the interior is pure Russian Orthodox. Visitors are welcome, but are asked to be respectful of worshipers. The cathedral is open to the public daily from 9 AM to 8 PM.

* Nevsky Prospekt - Extending southeast from Palace Square is Nevsky Prospekt, the main street of St. Petersburg, a once fashionable boulevard that is today reclaiming some of its former grandeur. During tsarist times, Nevsky Prospekt was home to the finest and most elegant shops in Saint Petersburg, as this boulevard catered to the rich. Today the buildings lining the street have been restored and many serve once again as shops and restaurants. One of the old building complexes has been modernized on its interior and turned into an upscale shopping center that includes a branch of Stockmann Department Store from Helsinki, showing that old and new can blend together without sacrificing the external appearance. Some cruise lines do offer what they call a "shopping tour," which in essence is a way to get you to be able to spend some free time in the city center that is focused upon Nevsky Prospekt. If you do not have access to a private car, driver and guide, this is a good option, as it enables you to spend a bit of free time in the heart of the city.

If of course you have a visa and feel comfortable using local transport, I highly recommend visiting this grand boulevard to be able to gain a feel for the commercial heart of Saint Petersburg.

* Palace Square and the Hermitage - The most striking feature of the old city center is Palace Square along the Neva River. The grandest building on the square is the Tsar's Winter Palace, a magnificent example of Russian baroque architecture. It was from Palace Square in October 1917 that the Bolsheviks stormed into the palace itself, bringing an end to the provisional government and setting into motion the era of Communist domination.

** The Hermitage, said to be the second greatest art gallery in the world after the Louvre in Paris. This is the most important part of the Winter Palace. The overall palace has more than 1,000 rooms as 117 separate staircases. Catherine the Great is credited with having brought the palace to its full grandeur through lavish spending on the building and its interior furnishings as well as its great art collection. The Hermitage was fortunately spared being destroyed or turned into government offices. Even the Communists recognized that it represented not only tsarist oppression, but also the grand history of the nation, and it was a valuable treasure for its artistic beauty. All through the Soviet Era, the building was maintained and open to the limited number of visitors that came to Leningrad. Since the fall of the Soviet Union, the Hermitage has undergone much restoration, some of it continuing to the present. It is considered to be the country's second greatest showcase after the Kremlin in Moscow. Yet visitors are surprised to find that on a warm to hot summer day, windows are open in the Hermitage. There is no air conditioning system and the valuable treasures are exposed to the outside air and humidity, something most museums containing priceless art would never permit. Because the building itself is also an architectural treasure, it would be exceptionally costly to literally rebuild the interior after installing a proper air conditioning and dehumidifying system. Apart from the cost, it would take a large labor force several years to totally rebuild the palace. Therefore no work has been done, and thankfully summer is a short season in Saint Petersburg. Opening hours are from 10:30 to 6 PM, Tuesday, Thursday, Saturday and Sunday. On Wednesday and Friday the museum keeps open until 9 PM. The museum is closed on Monday. Tickets can be purchased for early opening, but this must be done in advance and some cruise lines even offer an early opening tour, which gives you one hour before the full crowd arrives. Frankly even if you have a visa, attempting to visit on your own without prior ticket purchase can be exhausting, as you will wait several hours before gaining entry. It is best to visit the Hermitage as part of a group tour.

** Alexander Column, commemorating Russia's victory against Napoleon in 1812 stands in the middle of Palace Square. The angel atop the column symbolizes peace following the Napoleonic Wars.
** Palace Administrative Building stands on the south side of Palace Square. It was here that the civil servants of the Russian Empire did their work to run the government. Today this fully restored building serves as an office complex and has residential units and shops.

* Peter and Paul Fortress - Across the Neva River from the Winter Palace, occupying its own island stands the formidable Peter and Paul Fortress. It was built by Tsar Peter the Great in 1703, but was later used primarily as a prison by later Tsars. Initially the fortress was built to protect the city, since Russia and Sweden had been at odds over many Baltic territories. Within the fortress stands the imposing Peter and Paul Cathedral, where most of the Tsars and other royals since Peter the Great have been laid to rest. The most recent burial was in 2000 for Tsar Nicholas II and his entire family in a special room at the rear of the cathedral. Tickets must be purchased prior to entry, and the fortress is open from 8 AM to 5:40 PM daily except Wednesday.

* Petrogradsky Island is also a large residential district of the city that contains more upper and middle income apartment blocks. Its main boulevard is Kammennostrovsky Prospekt, which is home to many fine examples of Art Nouveau architecture from the late 19th century. The Imperial Naval Academy is to be found on Petrogradsky Island.

** Across from the academy, tied up along the bank of the river is the old battleship Aurora, which fired the opening shot of the October Revolution in 1917, and it can be visited It is open from 11 AM to 6 PM daily except Monday and Friday.

* Russian State Museum - Located inside the Mikhailovsky Palace, this museum features a massive collection of Russian fine art, crafts and sculpture. Unlike the Hermitage, it is seldom a focus of attention for foreign visitors and therefore is not nearly as crowded. Russian art, especially late 19th century impressionism, is superb and the finest works are exhibited in the state museum. It is open from 10 AM to 6 PM daily except Tuesday, with extended hours until 8 PM on Monday and 9 PM on Thursday. Tickets are purchased upon entering the building. The palace gardens are open with no charge from 10 AM until 10 PM daily. The gardens offer beautiful views of the domes of the Church of the Savior on Blood, which is adjacent.

* Saint Isaac's Cathedral - St. Petersburg possesses many glorious Russian Orthodox cathedrals, the two most noted being Saint Isaac's and the Church of the Savior on Blood. Saint Isaac's is the city's largest cathedral with its golden dome making the third largest in the world, but its architectural pattern speaks more to Western Europe than it does to the Russian tradition, but with its lavish use of gold and its icons covering the walls the interior is truly Russian Orthodox. The cathedral is open from 10:30 to 6 PM daily except it is closed Wednesday. Evening hours are 6 until 10:30 PM during summer, lasting through September, but Wednesday. Tickets must be purchased prior to entry.

* Saint Nicholas Naval Cathedral - This is still a working church in which services are held throughout the day. It is one of the most beautiful buildings in the city with its white and blue walls and golden domes. Visitors may enter most days unless a special ceremony is taking place. There is no charge and you are asked to be respectful and keep outside of the roped off area for worshipers. The cathedral is open daily from 7 AM to 7 PM.

* **Vasilevsky Island** - The two large islands north of the old city center are called Vasilevsky and Petrogradsky Islands. Each dates back to the 19th century and is home to a wide range of architectural styles for large apartment blocks that were built for both working class and merchant class families. The major cruise terminal where larger vessels dock is located on Vasilevsky Island, and you will be driving through it en route to various venues and in returning to the ship. Some smaller cruise ships will be docked along the Lieutenant Schmidt Embankment of the Great (Bolshaya) Neva River, which is on the southern edge of the island. The best known photo stop on Vasilevsky Island is the Strelka or split where the second branching of the Neva River occurs. The two Rostral Columns depict the rivers of Russia and served as lighthouses. The view to the Peter and Paul Fortress as well as the Hermitage makes this one of the most important photo stops in the city. And it is always congested with traffic since there are no designated parking areas. The Russian Institute of Art and Saint Petersburg University are housed on the eastern end of Vasilevsky Island leading to the Strelka. The Russian Institute of Art does have a student gallery open to the public for a nominal charge every day except Tuesday.

MY RECOMMENDATIONS FOR MINOR VENUES IN THE CITY (shown in alphabetical order):

* **Alexandrinsky Theater** - On Nevsky Prospekt, this is the city's other major performing arts center, built to resemble the famous Bolshoi Theater of Moscow. Many cruise lines will offer an evening performance here or at the Marinsky Theater, and it is a worthwhile experience.

* **Eleseevsky Gastronom** - This is one of the most elegant food shops in the world, and it dates back to tsarist times. During the Communist period it was allowed to remain open and serviced the high level party officials and their families. It is located on Nevsky Prospekt across the street from the Alexandrinsky Theater and easy to find because of its distinct Art Deco style. This incredible food shop is never seen on any ship sponsored guided excursion, but should be on your list if you are doing a private tour or going out on your own. You will be dazzled by its displays of fine quality food and it is hard to walk out without having made a purchase. It is open every day of the week from 10 AM to 11 PM.

* **Engineer's Castle, also known as Saint Michael's Castle** - This is a rather massive building set adjacent to the Summer Gardens. It was built for Tsar Paul I, but the tsar spent very little time here because he was assassinated 40 nights after occupying the castle. The story of this horrific event after so much went into the building of the castle is what is so fascinating to visitors. It is open daily from 10 AM to 6 PM but closed on Tuesday. Hours are extended until 9 PM on Thursday.

* **Field of Mars** - This great open park or parade ground dates back to the earliest years of the city as a place for military maneuvers. It affords a splendid view of the domes of the Church of the Savior on Blood. It also is home to a monument and eternal flame honoring the October Revolution. There is no charge to visit.

* Gostini Dvor - One of the city's oldest shopping arcades, it is not tourist oriented but it gives you a chance to become a part of everyday life. It is located on Nevsky Prospekt at Ulitsa Sadovaya and is a crossroads of several major Metro lines. Inside the arcade are small shops that are individually owned and sell just about everything imaginable. Its interior is like a gigantic maze, but it is fascinating and you can often find some good bargains on Russian made objects, including clothing, jewelry, household goods and a variety of vodkas, chocolates and other local snack foods. It is open daily from 10 AM to 10 PM and should not be missed.

* Marinsky Theater - The home of one of Russia's two great ballet companies, this 19th century theater is an architectural gem. Next door is the new and controversial modern theater of the same name. There are performances of opera and ballet during the summer and most cruise ships do offer an evening performance at the new or old Marinsky. It is a treat, as Russian ballet in particular is hard to match.

* Nine Hundred Day Siege Monument - Located at the far end of Moskovsky Prospekt in Victory Square, this breathtaking monument is a tribute to the million people who died during the Nazi siege of Leningrad and to the soldiers who protected the city from capture. Visiting is a very emotional experience, as it makes you ponder the great suffering of the people during World War II, and also the great loss of life. The exterior consists of a massive obelisk and many heroic bronze statues. Inside the amphitheater shaped bowl are eternal flames and plaques to the heroic defenders of the city, and finally underground is the actual museum for which there is a small entry fee. It is open from 11 AM to 6 PM Thursday to Monday, and from 11 AM to 5 PM on Tuesday. The monument is closed on Wednesday and the last Tuesday of each month. This is a very somber place and it is quite inspirational. It helps you appreciate the tremendous suffering of the residents of Leningrad during the war.

* Old Leningrad City Hall and Lenin Statue - Here you have a chance to see one of the largest statues of Lenin, set amid beautiful fountains. It will make you feel like you are back in the Soviet Era. It is located along Moskovsky Prospekt where Leninsky Prospekt begins. This is in the southern part of the city. Saint Petersburg is a city that revels in its grandeur, but this statue and old city hall complex is also a reminder of the country's Soviet history, as it was the birthplace of Vladimir Lenin and the Communist revolution. Because of Lenin's prominence, the great statue of him still stands in front of the former Leningrad City Hall, a building that was constructed during the Soviet Era. There are no opening hours since the great statue is outdoors. But the fountains are not always operational.

* Park Pobedy - A large park dedicated to honoring the great military heroes of the former Soviet Union, Park Pobedy's victory avenue lined with statues of the Soviet military heroes of World War II. Apart from walking the row of Soviet heroes, the park itself is quite large and has many paths that wind around its lakes. It is a nice respite from the busy city. The park is open daily in summer from 10 AM to 6 PM.

* Piskarovskoye Memorial Cemetery - Here is one of the most moving and somber of all monuments in Saint Petersburg. It is located in the northeastern part of the city in the Kalininsky District along Prospekt Nepokoronnykh. This memorial park, which is kept in an immaculate conditions, is the resting place for 0ver 400,000 Leningrad residents who lost their lives during the 900-Day Siege during World War II. With soft classical music playing and a massive bronze statue of Mother Russia looking down upon the grounds, you cannot help but be touched by the incredible sorrow that befell the city during the war. The memorial is open daily during summer from 9 AM to 9 PM. A visit here is in essence a way of paying respect to the sacrifices made by the residents of this city. It is hard to leave this monument without having tears in your eyes. It is a very moving experience.

* Summer Garden - These beautiful gardens also contain the very small palace that was home to Tsar Peter the Great during the early years of building Saint Petersburg. The gardens offer a very shady and cool respite from the city center, especially on a warm and humid day. The gardens are open from 10 AM to 9 PM daily during the summer months.

* Fabergé Museum - Located along the Fontanka Canal Embankment in the central city, this museum was once the home to the illustrious jeweler Karl Fabergé who is world famous for his masterful creations for the Russian Royal Family. During the height of tsarist rule, Saint Petersburg was considered to be the most opulent of European capitals, despite the fact that its masses lived in poverty. At one time, the French jeweler Fabergé had his studio and showroom on Nevsky Prospekt. He became world famous for his masterpiece jewel encrusted golden Easter eggs commissioned by the Tsars for their family. They were generally given as Easter gifts. These eggs were decorated in precious stones, and most opened up to reveal miniature scenes within. The home of Faberge has been recently opened as a museum, but to date none of the cruise lines have included it on their itineraries. Today many of them survive and are part of the 19th century treasures on display both in Saint Petersburg and Moscow. A few of the eggs have reached the art market, and when one on rare occasions comes up for auction, it generally fetches a price in the millions of dollars. You may visit the museum as part of a group tour or on your own. Unguided visits are allowed from 10 AM to 8:45PM daily while guided tours are conducted only until 6 PM.

* Yusupov Palace - This is one of many palaces that belonged to a noble family. But the Yusupov Palace, locted along the Moika River Canal is most famous because it was here that in 1917, Prince Yusupov arranged to murder the Siberian Monk named Rasputen. He was supposedly treating the Tsar's son for hemophilia and had the Tsarina under his influence. Many in court feared his influence and they detested is lecherous ways, so the Prince arranged to do him in. The grizzly story is told on visits to the palace and this is a very popular venue for those who love a good mystery. The palace is open from11 AM to 5 PM daily, but large tour groups mainly from the cruise lines crowd into the building all day long. It is difficult for anyone alone to be able to gain easy entry.

RECOMMENDATIONS OUTSIDE OF THE CITY (shown in alphabetical order):

* Catherine's Palace or Tsarskoye Selo (the proper Russian name) - This is a grand summer palace commissioned by Catherine the Great, located outside of the city by some 45 kilometers or 30 miles in the city of Pushkin. This lavish palace is a massive blue, white and gold building with equally magnificent gardens. The palace was totally destroyed during World War II, yet it was fully restored under the Communist regime because of its monumental importance. It is difficult to reach the palace without being on a group tour or having a car, driver and guide. And it is not practical to attempt to go without an escort guide because preference on entry is given to groups or those with individual guides. During summer the early opening is reserved only for tour groups. Individual hours are from Noon to 6:45 PM daily except Tuesday. The palace also has an excellent restaurant and entertainment is provided for group lunches.

* Kronstadt Island – This island in the middle of the Gulf of Finland is very historic, as it has served the role of being the naval base protecting the city from seaward invasion since shortly after its founding in 1704. The island became the modern naval base for the Baltic and North Sea fleet and after the Communist takeover and the creation of the Soviet Union, its significance increased. During the Cold War, it was off limits to foreign visitors. If you have a car and driver/guide you can visit Kronstadt. You would need to spend half a day to visit. You would traverse the great dam that protects the city, then visit the great cathedral, see the various World War II monuments and memorials and also be able to take close up pictures of any of the Russian Navy ships that happen to be in port at the time.

* Lake Ladoga and Doroga Zhisny - During World War II, the Red Army managed to get some supplies into the city during winter by maintaining at great effort a supply line across frozen Lake Ladoga. This massive lake, the largest in Europe, is just east of the city. Supplies were brought to help in the suffering during the 900-Day Siege. Today the road is marked every kilometer with a monument and there is a memorial arch at the lakeshore where the convoy reached land. Apart from its historic significance, the drive there and back is also quite scenic and gives a visitor a chance to see some of the Russian countryside.

* Pavlovsk Palace - The palace of Prince Paul, son of Catherine the Great is located close to Catherine's Palace. It was given to Prince Paul by the Empress to celebrate the birth of his first son, the future Alexander I. The actual building is nowhere near as grand as Catherine's Palace, but thought smaller, it is no less elegant. However, the massive grounds offer one of the largest and most beautiful park settings in all of greater St. Petersburg. It is open from 10 AM to 6 PM daily except the first Monday of each month. There is a separate admission for those who want to visit only the park.

* Peterhoff Palace or Petrodevoretz (the proper Russian name) - Built by Peter the Great, this smaller summer palace is no less magnificent on its interior. But it is best known for its incredibly designed exterior gardens. The palace is situated on a hill overlooking the Gulf of Finland. With the forces of gravity, Tsar Peter designed the elaborate water cascades and fountains that are graced by over 160 gold statues,

making this the Russian Versailles in every way. If you only have time to visit one of the two great palaces, my recommendation is for Peterhoff without hesitation. It is open during summer from 10:30 AM to 7 PM every day except Monday. The gardens are open under separate admission unless you buy a combined ticket. Garden hours are from 9 AM to 8 PM. The fountains are turned on at 11 AM with a musical fanfare that is quite spectacular and not to be missed. You can arrive by private car or on a motor coach tour. Priority entry into the palace is given to group tours. It is also possible to arrive or depart via a hydrofoil with direct access back to the docks along the Neva River near the Hermitage. Some group tours include this means of transport for one way.

Traveling to either of the three palatial estates or to Lake Ladoga enables visitors to get out into the countryside and sample a taste of rural Russia. Here small, unpainted wood farmhouses encircled by vegetable gardens stand as they once did in tsarist times. And in the small towns there are miniature versions of the great cathedrals, but built out of wood rather than stone or brick.

DINING OUT AND SAMPLING RUSSIAN CUISINE: Russian cuisine is based upon simple ingredients, as the peasants had little, partly out of poverty and partly because the land offers a limited bounty. But there was a creative spirit among Russian housewives, and the cuisine is surprisingly rich in variety. Root vegetables like beets and carrots are important, along with potatoes and cabbage and bits of meat when people could afford such a luxury. Fish is also a major element in the summer diet, especially sturgeon and salmon. And Russians love fish eggs that are salted and preserved - what we know as caviar. The finest quality is sturgeon roe from the Caspian Sea. But a less expensive red salmon caviar is also very popular.

Russian cooks were able to develop quite a varied and even elegant menu. In today's good restaurants such dishes as blini (filled crepes), perogi (stuffed dumplings), ukha (sturgeon, salmon and potato soup) and borsch (beet soup) are served to visitors as standard Russian fare. And to start of a great meal, one must sample Caspian Sea caviar along with traditional Russian vodka, which is quite strong. On most full day tours, especially out to the two summer palaces, lunch is generally included. And it is most often a traditional Russian lunch. But for those of you who have a visa or out on private tours, there are many fine restaurants from which to choose for lunch or dinner.

For those who will be sightseeing with a private car and driver/guide or those who have a visa and can go off on their own, I make the following restaurant recommendations, which are based upon my many years of enjoying the flavors of Russia (shown in alphabetical order):

* Dom Restauant – Located at Moika River Embankment # 72, this elegant Russian restaurant is just across the canal and south of St. Isaac' Cathedral. The extensive menu features a variety of traditional Russian dishes such as pelmeni, blini, borsch and many seafood and meat entrees. The hours of service are between Noon and 11:30 PM Monday thru Friday and 1 to 11:30 PM on weekends.

* **Eliseevsky Gastronom** - This is one of the most sumptuous food halls you have ever visited. It features breads, lunch meats, cheeses, caviar, smoked fish, glace fruits and nuts along with absolutely artistic pastries that are beyond description. It was opened in 1903 and during the Communist era it served the elite party members. You can have light sandwiches and desserts at the few tables in the center of the hall, but this is primarily a food emporium where you take home the goodies. It is an irresistible establishment located on Nevsky Prospekt one block south of Ulitsa Sadovaya and open from Noon until Midnight, and open from morning until late at night. No specific hours could be found.

* **Grand Europe Hotel Caviar Bar** – If you truly love genuine caviar and are willing to pay for it, this is where you should come. Every variety of quality Russian caviar is available and served in numerous ways with either fine champagne or vodka. The Caviar Bar is open daily from 5 to 11 PM and the hotel is one of the cornerstone buildings in the city center at the corner of Nevsky Prospekt and Mikhailovskaya Ulitsa.

* **Grand Europe Hotel main dining room** called L'Europe is a very elegant and favored place to dine for those who want the finest quality and service possible. The menu is very grand, as the name implies, featuring continental and Russian dishes served with impeccable style and grace. Breakfast is served between 7 and 10:30 AM, dinner between 6 and 11 PM Monday thru Saturday and a special brunch is available on Sunday 2 and 4:30 PM. The hotel is one of the cornerstone buildings in the city center at the corner of Nevsky Prospekt and Mikhailovskaya Ulitsa.

* **Katyusha Restaurant** – Located on Nevsky Prospekt # 24 in the city center, this very popular restaurant features an extensive menu filled with Russian favorites, European dishes and also vegetarian friendly cuisine. Both the food and atmosphere are very conducive to developing a strong sense of feeling for Russian culture. And the service is also excellent. The restaurant is open daily from Noon to 1 AM, and reservations are recommended, true to most good Russian restaurants.

* **Podvorye** – This is one of the best known restaurants among visitors who journey to the city of Pushkin and visit Catherine's Palace. Many tour operators who service the cruise industry use this restaurant for their lunch included tours. Podvorye is designed to resemble a Russian hunting lodge and to add to the atmosphere, they provide traditional entertainment. If you go on your own (reservations a must) you will choose from a very extensive traditional menu. But if you are part of a group tour, the meal will already have been predetermined. I have been told that when he is in Saint Petersburg, this is one of President Putin's favorite restaurants. I can personally say that the quality here is worthy of serving the president. The hours of service are between Noon and 11 PM daily.

* **Restoran** – Located adjacent to the university at Tamozhenny Lane # 21, this restaurant is virtually unknown to foreign tourists. Although close to where the small luxury cruise ships dock, it would be difficult to dine here even if you have a visa unless you have a guide, as English is hardly spoken. This restaurant caters more to the university population, but it is as authentic a neighborhood Russian

restaurant as you can find. Because so few tourist have visited, it is way down the list on Trip Advisor simply being unknown. But the food and service are excellent and you will be dining the way middle class Russians dine. I speak Russian, and find this to be a favorite because of its authenticity. If you come with a driver or guide, you will be treated to a rare experience that most fellow cruise ship passengers will not have had. The hours of service are from Noon to 11 PM daily.

* Russian Vodka Museum and Restaurant - Although the name sounds touristy, this is a popular venue with locals in Saint Petersburg. Yes there is a vodka museum, but it is the restaurant that is to me the primary feature. The decor is very simple, almost 19th century in its austerity. But the menu is extensive and the food is genuine Russian fare, well prepared and served by waiters who do speak good English. It is located near St. Isaak's Cathedral, great for those of you on smaller ships that will dock along the Neva River just a few blocks away. It is open from Noon to Midnight daily. And reservations are recommended, a basic trait in Russia. You receive a warmer welcome if you can say that you already have a reservation. The address is Konnogvardeyskiy Boulevard 4.

* Sadko - One of my favorite genuine Russian restaurants that although some tourists find with their guides, it is primarily a local favorite. The menu at Sadko is quite extensive and everything is prepared just as if you were eating in someone's grandmother's kitchen. Located opposite the Marinsky Theater on Ulitsa Glinka 2, and open from Noon to 1 AM. Reservations are recommended.

* Singer Cafe - This venerable cafe is found upstairs in the House of Books, which in Russian is Dom Knigi. Singer Cafe dates to the 19th century and has been a hangout for writers and artists even during the Soviet Era. It does get rather crowded during the lunch hour, but the sandwiches, blini and other traditional lunch dishes are superb, as are their amazing pastries. It is located on Nevsky Prospekt 28 on the second floor of Dom Knigi. Singer Cafe is open from 9 AM until 11 PM.

* Stolle – This popular Russian "fast food" restaurant has several locations across the city. Its most recognized restaurant is at Nevsky Prospekt # 11. Stolle is famous for its varied baked goods, among them are the meat and other savory pies, which are quite filling. My favorite, and a beloved dish in Russia is the savory cabbage pie. The mushroom pie is also another classic as are their sweet fruit pies. They also offer take away service. The restaurants open at 9 AM and close at 9 PM.

* Tsar - This is a must if you want a combination of an elegant Russian atmosphere combined with great traditional food. The atmosphere is like that of a private dining room in the tsar's palace. And the menu selections cover almost all aspects of great Russian dishes. It is located in the city center on Ulitsa Sadovaya 12, and open from Noon until Midnight. Reservations are recommended.

There are many other restaurants in the city that specifically cater to visitors, but the ones I have listed above are quite genuine and will give you a great Russian experience. I am sure that there are dozens, if not hundreds, of quality restaurants

I have not visited despite my 51 trips to Saint Petersburg. If nothing on my list appeals to you, ask your driver/guide for their recommendation.

SHOPPING: Unless you have a visa, it will be difficult to shop other than for souvenir items at shops or vendors where your tour operator chooses to stop. Among the souvenir items are the nested matrushka dolls and lacquer boxes. But be observant. Most are mass-produced and will sell anywhere from $20 to $200 depending upon size. However, if you want a genuine matruskha or box, it must be hand signed by the artist either on the bottom or for the box at one corner of the painted image. Genuine handmade dolls or boxes can cost anywhere from $100 for a very small one up into the thousands of dollars for the larger and more ornate dolls or boxes.

Amber jewelry is another gift item that many visitors purchase, but one must be careful, as fake amber is difficult to tell from the genuine article. Purchases should be made in a quality shop where some form of written guarantee is provided. But even then it is still a gamble. I would recommend that if you wish to purchase amber jewelry, wait until your ship visits Tallinn, Estonia, as the selection is much larger and the quality is higher.

Today visitors can buy small replicas of the famous Faberge eggs, or the hand painted wood eggs that were given among the peasant class. These are very traditional items that make nice moderately priced gifts. A real Faberge egg is beyond the reach of visitors, as they are so highly prized that if one does come up for auction, it sells for millions of Euro or dollars. And one item of note is the widespread sale of Soviet military medals; hats and other non-lethal souvenirs of the former military might from the Communist Era. Many are genuine, but there are also a lot of reproductions, so once again buyer beware.

There are several shops for both the souvenir merchandise as well as for clothing, accessories and decorative objects d'art that I feel comfortable in noting in this book. My recommendations include:

* Bolshoi Gostiny Dvor - The main shopping arcade on Nevsky Prospekt 35, with its own Metro stop underneath, this is a virtual maze of arcades lined with individual shops that sell just about everything from food to cosmetics, food items, housewares, gifts and even souvenirs. It dates to the late 19th century and is very typically Russian. It is open from 10 AM to 10 PM daily.

* Galeria Shopping Mall - Across from Stockman you will find a very modern yet traditionally Russian shopping mall with over 290 shops and restaurants. This is quite a massive establishment and worthy of your visit. It is located on Ligovsky Prospekt 30A,. It is open daily from 10 AM to 11 PM, but restaurants inside the mall close at 8 PM daily.

* Kuznechny Market - This is one of the largest public food markets in Saint Petersburg, and some cruise lines actually bring guests here for a look and to sample some of the take out foods. The market offers produce, meat, fish, cheese, honey,

dried fruits and nuts as well as baked goods. It is a fascinating place to visit. Located at Dostoyevskaya Ploschtad and can be reached on the Metro through Vladimirskaya Station. It is open from 8 AM to 8 PM daily, but closes at 7 PM on Sunday.

* Red October - This is a highly reputable and extensive gift shop that sells Russian arts and crafts from the low priced matrushka dolls all the way up to one of a kind original dolls and lacquer boxes along with very high-quality amber jewelry. They also have a free vodka bar, but be careful as a few vodka shots and you may buy more than you desired. They also have a large selection of caviar. Located at Konnogvardeiskiy Boulevard 6, just up the street from the Russian Vodka Museum.

* Stockmann Department Store - The well-known Helsinki mercantile has opened a beautiful new store at Nevsky Prospekt 114-116,. This five-story store is not as large as the main store in Helsinki, but it carries a wide variety of merchandise including some Russian brands. The store is open from 10 AM to 11 PM daily.

FINAL WORDS: Whether you have a visa or are required to participate in ship's tours, you will come away from Saint Petersburg with a new understanding of Russia. You will also bring away memories of a grand city that saw its share of turmoil and war, but one that has now risen again to recapture some of its old imperial glory. In my years of cruising and lecturing on the Baltic ports of call, I have never met a ship's guest who was not enchanted with Saint Petersburg. Some guests found that they were not comfortable being in Russia and felt that they were either being watched by government minders while the majority found the people to be surprisingly friendly and warm. It is a matter of whether you are fully open to a new experience without any preconceived perceptions. Given a chance, the Russian people will show you that we are not all that different.

Saint Petersburg is a great city, historic, vibrant and expanding as part of its role as a great cultural center for the new Russia. A visit to Saint Petersburg should be viewed as a great treat and as a chance to see what life in Russia is really like. You will find it most revealing.

SAINT PETERSBURG MAPS

THE CENTRAL CITY

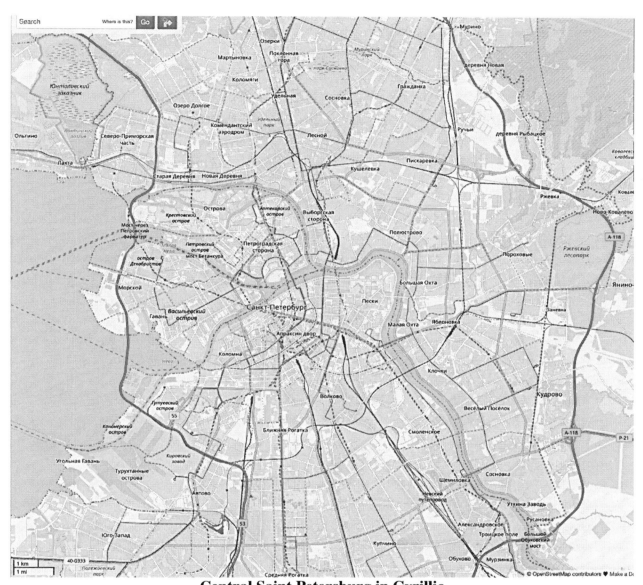

Central Saint Petersburg in Cyrillic

This map is best viewed directly from OpenStreetMap.com on your personal device where it can be expanded or one specific area can be enlarged. Given the format of this book, it is impossible to display maps with the level of detail you might wish to have while actually out exploring the city. But the OpenStreetMap maps used directly are the tool I always rely upon.

INNER SAINT PETERSBURG

The inner heart of Saint Petersburg

This map is best viewed directly from OpenStreetMap.com on your personal device where it can be expanded or one specific area can be enlarged. Given the format of this book, it is impossible to display maps with the level of detail you might wish to have while actually out exploring the city. But the OpenStreetMap maps used directly are the tool I always rely upon.

THE NEVA RIVER IN THE CITY CENTER

Along the main channel of the Neva River

This map is best viewed directly from OpenStreetMap.com on your personal device where it can be expanded or one specific area can be enlarged. Given the format of this book, it is impossible to display maps with the level of detail you might wish to have while actually out exploring the city. But the OpenStreetMap maps used directly are the tool I always rely upon.

THE SOUTHERN SUBURBS

Along Moskovsky Prospekt

This map is best viewed directly from OpenStreetMap.com on your personal device where it can be expanded or one specific area can be enlarged. Given the format of this book, it is impossible to display maps with the level of detail you might wish to have while actually out exploring the city. But the OpenStreetMap maps used directly are the tool I always rely upon.

THE NORTHERN SUBURBS

The newly developing Primorsky District

This map is best viewed directly from OpenStreetMap.com on your personal device where it can be expanded or one specific area can be enlarged. Given the format of this book, it is impossible to display maps with the level of detail you might wish to have while actually out exploring the city. But the OpenStreetMap maps used directly are the tool I always rely upon.

The typical Taiga landscape around Saint Petersburg

The countryside like a scene from "Dr. Zhivago

Sailing up the Neva River past Vaselivsky Island

The first bridge on the Neva River looking into the heart of the city

Palace Square is the heart of Saint Petersburg

The Hermitage or Winter Palace of the Tsars

The grand throne of the Russian Tsar inside the Hermitage

St. Isaac's Cathedral – Largest in Russia

Church of the Savior on Blood seen from the Field of Mars

Façade of the Church of the Savior on Blood

Our Lady of Kazan Cathedral on Nevsky Prospekt

Cathedral of Peter and Paul inside the old fortress

St. Nicholas Cathedral of the Fishermen

Alexandrovsky Gardens along the Bolshaya Neva River

The Bronze Horseman – Peter the Great looking out over the Neva

Along the Griboyedova Canal looking to the Church of the Savior on Blood

Russian State Museum of Art – Mikhailovsky Palace

The famous Marinsky Theater

Walking along famous Nevsky Prospekt

Nevsky Prospekt is the grandest boulevard in Saint Petersburg

The incredible elegance of the Eleseivski Gastronom on Nevsky Prospekt

The Lenin statue is a reminder of the Soviet Era

Apartment blocks are a reminder of the Soviet Era

The Piscerova Cemetery is a reminder of the Nazi 900 -day siege in WWII

A small sampling of the new high-rise southern suburbs of Saint Petersburg

New upscale apartments in northern Primorsky District

PETRODEVORTEZ AND PETERHOFF PALACE

The Peterhoff Palace area

This map is best viewed directly from OpenStreetMap.com on your personal device where it can be expanded or one specific area can be enlarged. Given the format of this book, it is impossible to display maps with the level of detail you might wish to have while actually out exploring the city. But the OpenStreetMap maps used directly are the tool I always rely upon.

PUSHKIN AND CATHERINE'S PALACE

Tsarskoye-Selo, Catherine's Palace

This map is best viewed directly from OpenStreetMap.com on your personal device where it can be expanded or one specific area can be enlarged. Given the format of this book, it is impossible to display maps with the level of detail you might wish to have while actually out exploring the city. But the OpenStreetMap maps used directly are the tool I always rely upon.

The grandeur of the gardens at Peterhoff Palace

The Peterhoff gold fountains seen from the palace terrace

The incredible gardens of Pavlovsk Palace in Pushkin

The magnificent Catherine's Palace façade

The chapel tower at Catherine's Palace

The golden grand ballroom at Catherine's Palace

TALLINN, ESTONIA

A map of greater Tallinn, Estonia. (© OpenStreetMap contributors)

At the start of the century if you would have told someone you were going on a cruise and the ship was visiting Tallinn, most people would have asked, "where's that?" As Baltic Sea cruises have gained popularity in the past 15 years, Tallinn has become one of highlights after Saint Petersburg, its story book Old Town being the major feature that visitors find so captivating.

ABOUT ESTONIA: Estonia is a very small country, covering 45,099 square kilometers or 17,413 square miles. It is about the size of Denmark, but it only has a population of 1,400,000 people. The flag of Estonia, which has three horizontal stripes, blue, black and white in that order, symbolizes the physical geography of the nation. The blue represents the Baltic Sea on which Estonia borders, the black is symbolic of the dark soil that nourishes the people and some say the white stands for the snows of winter, others say for purity. This small country emerged out of the former Soviet Union in 1991 and is doing quite well economically despite its small population. And its capital city of Tallinn is one of the most visited ports on the Baltic Sea apart from Saint Petersburg, Russia.

THE NATURAL SETTING: Estonia is the product of the last ice age. As glaciers retreated, they deposited small areas of fine till, which became Estonia's deep, rich soil, but many parts of the nation are rather rocky and bare, as the glaciers stripped the land to bedrock. The glacial ice also pockmarked the land, leaving behind over 1,500 small lakes. Likewise, as sea level rose, many shoreline areas were flooded, giving Estonia over 800 islands.

The land is thickly forested in a mix of broadleaf deciduous and coniferous trees, presenting a verdant landscape. It is essentially the same landscape surrounding Helsinki and Saint Petersburg, what the Russians call taiga. A significant portion of the forest has been cleared over the centuries for agricultural use.

The Estonian climate is identical to that of southern Finland and the region that surrounds Saint Petersburg. Summers are cool and very mild, punctuated by rain showers. Winters are long with more darkness than daylight, and cold with plenty of snowfall. This is definitely a harsh climate, but one that has in some way helped to shape the rugged Estonian personality.

A BRIEF LOCAL HISTORY: The history of Estonia is linked to that of its other two Baltic Sea neighbors, Latvia and Lithuania. All three have spent the greater part of their existence dominated over by the larger powers surrounding them, in particular by Imperial Russia and of late the Soviet Union.

The people of Estonia have lived in their homeland for at least 5,000 years. Their ancestors are related to those of Finland, as this is one of the other two Baltic nations that speak a Uralic or Finno Ugric language. The Estonian and Finnish tongues are very closely related, and given their close proximity, they have exceptionally close socio-economic ties. High-speed hydrofoil service enables one to travel between the two capital cities in approximately one hour. Car and passenger ferryboats also ply back and forth on a frequent schedule that takes a bit longer. Many Finns cross over to Tallinn to shop, especially for beer or vodka because the prices are so much lower in Estonia as a result of lower taxation. And now there is no currency exchange issue since Estonia did join the Eurozone.

Early Estonian history saw the country as a part of the Danish Empire from 1219 until it was literally sold to the Teutonic Knights in 1346. The Swedish Empire conquered the territory in 1561 and held it until Russia under Peter the Great began to expand its Baltic coastline in 1721. Russian domination lasted for two centuries until the country broke free during the Russian Revolution of 1917. To the present day, the Russian language is widely spoken and one still sees signs written in the Cyrillic script. This is primarily due to Estonia having seen forced movement of Russians to dominate the country's industries when it was a part of the Soviet Union. Estonia's population is 30 percent Russian thanks to that forced migration during the Soviet Era. This has presented problems since independence, as the Estonian majority still feels a degree of enmity toward Russians because of the years of Soviet domination. And some worry that this could prompt Russia to someday invade to protect their brethren, as was the case with Crimea and is still simmering between Russia and the Ukraine. I personally do not believe their worries are valid, especially with Estonia being a member of both the European Union and NATO. Any military action against Estonia would have to be met by NATO force otherwise the alliance would crumble.

After the Russian Revolution, all three of the Baltic States declared their independence. But the Germans occupied the country in 1918, uniting it with Latvia. With the end of World War I, Estonian independence was restored in 1919. The country's political scene was not very stable, going through 11 changes of government between 1921 and 1931. However, Soviet occupation in 1940, ended independence, the Russians taking the country at a time when the German forces were occupying France, thus the West paid no heed to Estonia. When Hitler abruptly terminated his peace pact with Russia in 1941, Nazi forces rolled through the Baltic States on their march toward Leningrad, thus putting Estonia under harsh German rule until the Soviet Union pushed them out in 1944. From then on, the country remains a part of the Soviet Union and experienced renewed ethnic subjugation despite having been declared the Estonian Soviet Socialist Republic. This condition was true in the two other Baltic States. They existed in name only but their governments were dominated by loyal Communist Party leaders most of who were Russian.

Since gaining its independence in 1991 with the collapse of the Soviet Union, Estonia has shown a remarkable ability to thrive. The country's economy is a mix of agriculture, timber and textile manufacturing. Agriculture is limited by the lack of sizeable areas with good soil. The country is known for its fine dairy products and summer fruit orchards. The only significant grains that Estonia is capable of growing are oats and rye, thus the national breads are of a rather heavy and coarse texture, as is true in much of Russia. Trade with the western nations of Europe and increasing tourism, especially from the cruise industry have given the economy a significant boost. And financial services and electronics also play a major role. Estonia has little foreign debt and its government generally operates on a balanced budget. The ratio of public debt to the gross domestic product is the lowest within the European Union, which it joined in 2004 and today it is also a member of the Eurozone. The country is also a member of the North Atlantic Treaty Organization, one of the first remnants of former Soviet domination to join.

THE PHYSICAL LAYOUT OF THE CITY OF TALLINN: The national capital is Tallinn, a city whose greater area population of 500,000 makes it the largest city in the country, containing nearly 35 percent of the national total. Tallinn occupies relatively level ground that wraps around a wide bay extending in from the Gulf of Finland. There are a few small glacial lakes around Tallinn, the largest being just to the southeast of the main city core. And on the margins of the city the land does show some degree of undulation with moderate size hills. But the most impressive feature is the hill close to the shoreline upon which the original town started to develop in medieval times. This is what is today called Old Tallinn, an almost totally walled in city with two distinct sections. Most of it is just very slightly above the level of the surrounding land and is called Lower Old Town. Then there is an abrupt scarp that causes a small knob to rise up about 30 meters or 100 feet above the rest of its surroundings. This has become known as Upper Old Town and is where once the aristocracy lived. The major portion of the wall system has remained intact, but a portion was destroyed during World War II and not rebuilt. But it is still safe to call Old Tallinn a walled city,

New Tallinn spreads both east and west of Old Tallinn and has fairly regular streets that do not twist and turn too greatly, although it cannot be called a grid pattern. And then to the south the city stretches for several kilometers along a few arterial streets. There are no major expressways and essentially traffic is light and there is more the feel of an overgrown town than that of a large city. On several of the streets there are trams that provide the only major form of public transit apart from busses.

The city shows all the signs of being a part of the dynamic lifestyle of modern Europe with Internet cafes, people carrying cell phones and an array of beautiful new shops in its downtown. But Old Tallinn, largely unchanged with its cobblestone streets and buildings dating to medieval times, is the gem that visitors come to see. Many buildings also represent post medieval development during the Hanseatic League, when Estonia served as a major trading center between the east and west. The city of Tallinn, as the focal hub of Estonian culture, was under alternate domination of Denmark and Sweden during much of its medieval history. By the early 1700's, Estonia fell under the domination of Russia, and despite its brief sojourn into the realm of independent states during the 1919 to 1941 period; the influence of Russia has been the strongest of any outside factors. Surprisingly though there is little architectural influence in Old Tallinn given that Estonia always traded with the West. The architecture of the older parts of Tallinn show more Germanic or Scandinavian influences than Russian. Because of the strong ties to Denmark and Sweden prior to being absorbed into the Russian Empire, Old Town Tallinn's buildings look more like those you would find in Copenhagen or Stockholm, with steeply pitched roofs tiled in slate, multi-pane windows and richly adorned facades plastered over and painted in muted pastel colors. The Old Town constitutes the heart of Tallinn, and today it can often be so crowded with tourists when four to five cruise ships descend upon its port at the same time. This may be profitable for the local merchants, but it can be a bit maddening for the visitor. If you are exceptionally lucky, your ship will be the only one in port. I have experienced this on several occasions. Most of the time during summer there can be three to as many as five mid to large size cruise ships in port at the same time. And you can well how congested the Old Town becomes.

SEEING THE SIGHTS IN TALLINN: Cruise ships all have shuttle bus service to the center of the city, parking just about two blocks away from the main gate into the Old Town. Most visitors walk the streets of Old Town, either on their own or through ship sponsored walking tours.

There is a hop on hop off bus, but it can only take visitors around the outside of the Old Town wall, stopping atop Tompea Hill in the Upper Old Town where there is a small parking area. The hop on hop off bus does, however, take visitors to several interesting sites in the modern city, some of which do date back to Tsarist times.

In all honesty, having a private car and driver for the day is an extravagant expense because the city is compact and by walking or using the local streetcar or hop on hop off bus, you can visit all of the major venues. For me to say this is significant, as I normally favor the use of a private car and driver/guide.

Unlike other Baltic cities, hiring a taxi for sightseeing is a bit difficult since so few of the drivers speak English. However, those who do congregate near the docks where cruise ships are anchored will be able to speak a bit of English. But even in this case, only a handful are proficient enough to conduct a tour of the city.

Because Tallinn is so small, the old and new cities are side-by-side. Walking is the best way to see both the Old Town and the adjacent newer shopping area. The weather is most often cool, and there are plenty of cafes where one can take a rest.

The Lower Old Town occupies the small hill overlooking the harbor, and it is accessible from the ship on foot although most cruise lines provide shuttle bus service for those who do not elect to go on a tour. In 1944, when the Red Army advanced on Tallinn to drive out the Germans, there was significant shelling and many buildings were badly damaged or destroyed. Since the war, ongoing restoration has removed those scars, as the people rebuilt Old Town with loving care, because to the Estonians, this small section of the city was their pride and joy.

The city has two palaces. Peter the Great built Kadriorg Palace as a summer retreat for his wife, located outside the old walled city and to the east of the present modern downtown. The government is today housed in Old Town in the former palace of the Russian duke who ruled during Imperial times. It is located in Upper Old town, which is atop Tompea Hill, the highest natural feature in the entire city. The old Imperial Palace is today the seat of the Estonian government and is rarely open to the public.

There are numerous magnificent Lutheran churches and the dominant Russian Orthodox Cathedral. The Saint Mary's Church (Lutheran) and the Alexander Nevsky Cathedral (Orthodox) are the city's highest landmarks in Old Town. And facing the market square of Old Town is the medieval Town Hall of Tallinn with its tall, but narrow stone tower. These are the major landmark buildings, as Tallinn was never a major center of power, primarily having been a vassal state during most of its history. Tallinn is, however, one of the oldest cities in the region, its actual origins beginning in the 10th century. All of the important landmarks that represent the earlier growth of the city are found in the Old Town, radiating down from Toompea Hill where an ancient limestone fortress was built in the 10th century, but only the battlements and wall remain.

It has only been since 1991 that the country has seen the rapid economic development resulting from becoming an integrated member of the Baltic community. Tallinn has experienced significant growth, yet still retains the flavor of a small city because that is what it truly is. The city center of modern Tallinn is sprouting beautiful ultra-modern high-rise office towers that are very reminiscent of North American cities, reminding me somewhat of Halifax, Nova Scotia in eastern Canada. No other Baltic Sea city possesses a downtown skyline that is as modern and has as many tall buildings as found in Tallinn. Likewise, the city center has two major department stores, one of which is linked to a large shopping mall. Within the central portion of the city, there is a lot of remodeling of older buildings, demolition of those unworthy of restoration, and there is a lot of new construction, showing that Tallinn is a city going places economically.

The residential areas reflect both the Soviet Era with rather grim apartment blocks, but not of the magnitude seen in larger cities in Russia. And today many of those reminders of the Soviet Era are either being remodeled or replaced. There were always private family residences, and today that trend can be seen in the leafy suburbs of Tallinn along with modern glass fronted apartment blocks that would be considered upmarket.

Tallinn has distinct neighborhoods that represent different eras in its growth. In the far southern suburb of Nõmme, one can see beautiful houses that date back to the interwar years when Estonia briefly flourished. In Kadriorg, the tree-lined streets reflect the grand era of the Tsars, when Estonian and Russian aristocrats held the power of the country in their hands. But the Lasnamäe district reflects the drab block-like apartment complexes built during the Soviet era. Despite the ugliness of the Soviet influenced architecture, people in Estonia today have allowed their negative feelings regarding Communist rule to diminish, and the country maintains an active trade with its giant neighbor Russia.

The only way to visit any of these neighborhoods, for those who are interested in residential architecture, would be through having a private car or hiring a taxi, as the tour busses do not generally include purely suburban districts as part of a tour. However, keep in mind that few taxi drivers speak much English, if any. A few city tours will include a visit to the Kadriorg Palace, thus the route you will take shows some of the beautiful wood villas that were built by Russian aristocrats.

The most important sights to see in Tallinn are confined to two small areas of the city. The best way to get around is to take one of your ship's official tours, as this will afford you the services of a licensed guide. But it is also easy to walk the Old City on your own, however, you will miss a few of the sights in the newer, more modern city. The most important sights to be seen in Tallinn are detailed below with any exhibiting a double asterisk being a venue within the confines of the site listed above (major sites listed in alphabetical order with secondary sites within a major site shown underneath with two asterisks):

* Kadriorg Palace - Built by Peter the Great for his wife's summer enjoyment, today this is a classic example of Russian imperial architecture. Today the palace is part museum and part home to the President of Estonia. The park and gardens are now open to the public where once they were reserved for the Tsarina. This is the only major venue not within walking distance of where the ship's shuttle busses drop off guests. It is necessary to take a taxi to visit the Kadriorg Palace, and numerous taxis will be found throughout the city center. The hop on hop off busses also start their

routes where the ship shuttle busses drop off passengers, and Kadriorg Palace is on their circuit. Tickets are available at the palace. Opening hours are from 10 AM to 6 PM Tuesday, Thursday thru Sunday and Wednesday has extended hours until 8 PM. The palace is closed on Monday.

* Lennusadam Seaplane Harbor - For those who have a maritime and aviation interest, this is a very large and impressive base for seaplane operations. This is not considered to be one of the main tourist attractions, but it is on the hop on hop off bus route. The facility is open Tuesday thru Sunday from 10 AM to 6 PM and guided tours are offered.

* Lower Old City - It is simply a matter of walking the small quarter that is contained within one of the best-preserved walls in Europe. Old City Tallinn contains a beautiful main square with a grand town hall that dates to medieval times. There are also many buildings that show the typical Hanseatic facades from the days when Tallinn was linked to this major trading league. The Lower Old City is home to the town square which fronts on the old town hall. The square is filled with many restaurants offering a mix of cuisines.

** Kiek in de Kök - This giant round tower built in 1475 was the main battlement tower for the defense of Old Tallinn. Today it and the museum offer a look at the ancient history of the city. The museum is open from 10 AM to 5:30 PM daily.

* Opera House and Concert Hall - Located in the new downtown area, opposite the main square that is just across from the main entry gate into the Old Town, these two beautiful buildings date back to the late Russian imperial period. These facilities are only open when performances are being held and therefore during most days can only be viewed from the outside. They are side by side and face the main entry gate into the Lower Old Town opposite the park.

* Tallinn Song Festival Grounds - This outdoor musical venue was where the Estonians expressed their desire for freedom from Soviet domination through song and not violence. If on your own, the song festival grounds can be reached on the hop on hop off bus or via a short taxi ride. The grounds are on the eastern side of the waterfront from the downtown area. Opening hours are from 9 AM to 5 PM daily.

* Tallinn TV Tower - This tall broadcasting tower has both an observation deck and restaurant. It is 314 meters tall, which is approximately 1,000 feet, making it the tallest structure in Estonia. People come for the views on a clear day, as it is possible to look across the Gulf of Finland and with binoculars you can see the skyline of Helsinki, Finland. The tower is well to the east of the city center, and it is rarely included on ship tours. The TV tower is on the hop on hop off bus route to the eastern suburbs. It is open daily from 10 AM to 7 PM, but should only be visited on a clear day otherwise you waste time and money. When it is clear, the view is incredible.

* Upper Old City - The upper Old City is home to the large Saint Mary's Lutheran

cathedral with its wood coats of arms on the interior walls and the Russian Orthodox Alexander Nevsky Cathedral along with the Toompea Castle that was home to the Russian viceroy during the period of imperial occupation.

** Alexander Nevsky Cathedral - You may enter the cathedral only when services are not being held.

** Lookout Points - To the west of the cathedral and palace are two lookout points that provide an excellent view of the lower Old City and the skyline of the modern city beyond. Today that palace is home to the Estonian Parliament.

** Saint Mary's Cathedral - This is the city's great Lutheran cathedral, which is the dominant faith of Estonia. The cathedral and its bell tower are open to visitors from 10 AM to 3:30 PM daily except Monday.

** Toompea Castle - The castle is today the seat of government and tours are given daily Monday thru Thursday from 10 AM to 4 PM for groups of up to 35 people. Tours are offered in English, Estonian and Russian.

SHOPPING: Finnish visitors love to come and shop for clothing, accessories and household goods because of lower taxes that translate to lower prices. You will find Scandinavian and German brands of high quality, so if you are interested in adding to your wardrobe or looking for gift items for the home, then Tallinn is a good place to shop. There are two major malls and two major department stores in the city center of Tallinn:

* Kaubamaja Department Store - This is an Estonian department store located in the heart of the city, attached to the Viru Shopping Mall. This store offers a wide variety of clothing, accessories, toiletries and housewares that are all of high quality. And in clothing and household linens it features some very high style with a unique local sense of design. Kaubamaja does represent what I would consider higher end shopping with a unique Estonian sense of style. The store is open seven days a week from 9 AM to 9 PM.

* Solaris Mall - Located across from the main entrance to the Opera House, this mall offers a variety of excellent shops featuring clothing, footwear, health and beauty aids, jewelry, books and a full-service supermarket. There are also numerous restaurants and a multiplex cinema inside the mall. The mall is open from 9 AM to 11 PM daily, but shops are only open from 10 AM to 9 PM, but restaurants stay open until 11 PM as does the grocery store.

* Stockmann Department Store - This is a branch of the famous Stockmann of Helsinki. It is much smaller and does not have the great selection you will find in Helsinki, but it still is a major store with plenty to choose from. It has a complete line of clothing, accessories, household goods and a grocery department. Stockmann is a few blocks from the Viru Shopping Mall, next to the Swissotel. The store is open from 9 AM to 9 PM daily, but on Sunday it does not open until 10 AM.

* Viru Shopping Mall - located across the park from the main gate into the Lower Old City. The mall is the largest in the city center and it is attached to the high-rise Viru Hotel. And Kaubamaja Department Store is a part of the mall. The mall also includes 109 shops, a major bookseller that has a large selection of English language books and a full service supermarket, The mall is open daily from 9 AM to 9 PM.

ESTONIAN CUISINE: The cuisine of Estonia is worth sampling. Like all Baltic Sea countries, it is heavily oriented toward fish and seafood along with fresh vegetables. The breads are very dark, as in Russia and Finland, but the Estonian version is softer and sweeter. It is delicious with fresh butter. Vegetable and fish soups are also very popular, as are many varieties of fish generally baked. There are numerous restaurants in the Old City and they are especially busy on days when multiple ships are in port. Over the years I have found one Old City restaurant located on the town square to be consistently good. And I also have a favorite that is not in the Old City. I hereby recommend the following restaurants (shown in alphabetical order):

* Finlandia Caviar Tallinn – This unique caviar and oyster restaurant is located in the Lower Old Town at Vaike Karja # 1 not far from the main gate. This restaurant is devoted to the finest quality Russian and Scandinavian caviar and fresh oysters served in a variety of ways. They also have tasting plates where you can sample various types of caviar and oysters. The prices are high, but if you love either genuine caviar or high-quality oysters, it is well worthwhile paying the price. They are open Monday thru Thursday Noon to 9 PM, Friday and Saturday Noon to 10 PM and Sunday Noon to 6 PM. Why not treat yourself if this is something you crave. This is the part of the world where it is at its best.

* Kaerajaan - Located on the old town square at Raekoja plats 17, this is a superb restaurant that offers modern versions of traditional Estonian cuisine. Surprisingly it is not as highly rated on Trip Advisor as many other Old City restaurants, but I have always found it consistently good year after year and everyone I have suggested it many guests have always come back and told me how much they enjoyed it. You can dine indoors or outdoors depending upon the weather. They are open from 10 AM to 11 PM.

* Kohvik Komeet - Located in the ultra-modern Solaris Mall, this restaurant with its wrap around windows offers a great view of the Old City and the Opera House. It is on the fourth floor of the mall, reached by elevator. The food is superb and their pastries are beyond belief. They have a variety of delicious soups, hot and cold entrees, good salads and of course you must save room for dessert. The restaurant is open for breakfast, lunch and dinner and you can always come just for their incredible pastries. It is open daily from 10 AM to 11 PM. Few, if any tourists ever venture here on their own and they are missing one of the best dining experiences in Tallinn.

* Lido - Also located in the Solaris Mall, this restaurant is part of a chain found in Scandinavia and the Baltic States. Lido is a buffet style restaurant that offers an incredible variety of dishes with local flavor. And in true Estonian fashion, they also

offer outstanding, decadent desserts. It is open daily from 10 AM to 11 PM. Again this is a restaurant that few tourists will ever discover on their own.

* Rataskaevu 16 – Located in the Lower Old Town just a block west of the Old Town Hall at Rataskaevu # 16, this is one of the most popular restaurants among visitors to the walled city. The menu is quite diverse and features Estonian, Russian and Scandinavian dishes served in a very historic setting. The quality of the cuisine and the service are both excellent. Because of its fine reputation, it is recommended that you have your cruise ship travel desk book a table in advance. Their hours of service are Noon to Midnight Monday thru Friday and Noon to 11 PM on weekends.

* Vaike Rataskaevu 16 – Located in the Lower Old Town at Niguliste # 6, half a block west of the Tallinn Information Center. You will find that this is another very highly recommended restaurant and has been a favorite of visitors for several years. The menu consists of Estonian and Scandinavian cuisine, with fresh fish being a specialty. The quality of the cuisine and the level of service are both outstanding. Their hours of service are Noon to 11 PM Sunday thru Thursday and Noon to 11:45 PM Friday and Saturday.

FINAL WORDS: The people of Tallinn are gracious and friendly, and among the younger generation English is widely spoken. This is a very clean city and has an exceptionally low crime rate. Thus, venturing out on one's own is totally safe. If you do not take a group tour, feel free to walk around both the Old City and the modern city center.

Today the city of Tallinn is experiencing a summertime invasion by the cruise industry. In the last few years, a new wharf had to be added to accommodate the mega cruise ships, as all of the major lines bring visitors to Tallinn. There are times when as many as five ships can be in port on a given day, with most guests intent upon visiting the old town. Such crowds do take away from the enjoyment of the port, but are welcomed by the merchants and restaurants because of the revenue being generated. It is recommended that after spending a couple of hours in the Old Town that one is better off taking a taxi or hop on hop off bus to the Kadriorg Palace and Gardens and then exploring the adjacent neighborhood of 18th and 19th century Russian homes of former nobles. And then a visit to the city center can be quite rewarding because it affords a look at everyday commercial life. For those who wish to venture afar, bicycle rentals or the use of taxis will enable you to visit more of the city than just its core area. I also recommend spending an hour walking around the modern downtown core of Tallinn to see how prosperous and progressive it is. The modern downtown reflects the new role of Estonia within the European Union as a progressive country that is on the cutting edge architecturally.

TALLINN MAPS

THE CENTRAL CITY

Central Tallinn

This map is best viewed directly from OpenStreetMap.com on your personal device where it can be expanded or one specific area can be enlarged. Given the format of this book, it is impossible to display maps with the level of detail you might wish to have while actually out exploring the city. But the OpenStreetMap maps used directly are the tool I always rely upon.

THE HEART OF TALLINN

The heart of the city

This map is best viewed directly from OpenStreetMap.com on your personal device where it can be expanded or one specific area can be enlarged. Given the format of this book, it is impossible to display maps with the level of detail you might wish to have while actually out exploring the city. But the OpenStreetMap maps used directly are the tool I always rely upon.

THE HISTORIC OLD TOWN

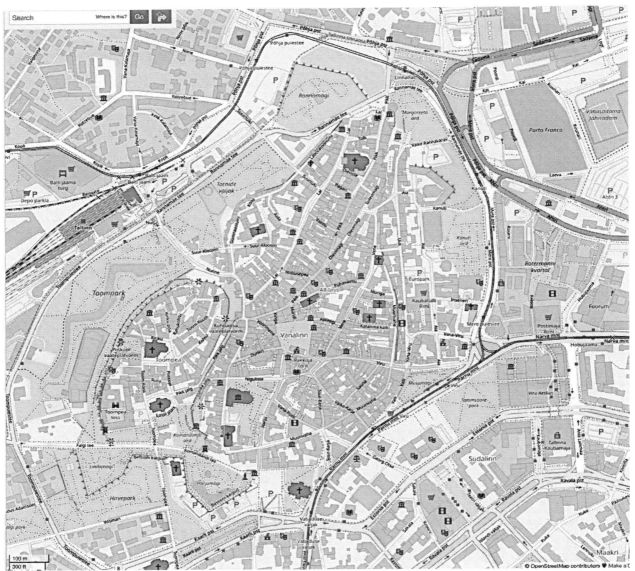

Old Town and part of the downtown

This map is best viewed directly from OpenStreetMap.com on your personal device where it can be expanded or one specific area can be enlarged. Given the format of this book, it is impossible to display maps with the level of detail you might wish to have while actually out exploring the city. But the OpenStreetMap maps used directly are the tool I always rely upon.

KADRIOG PALACE AREA

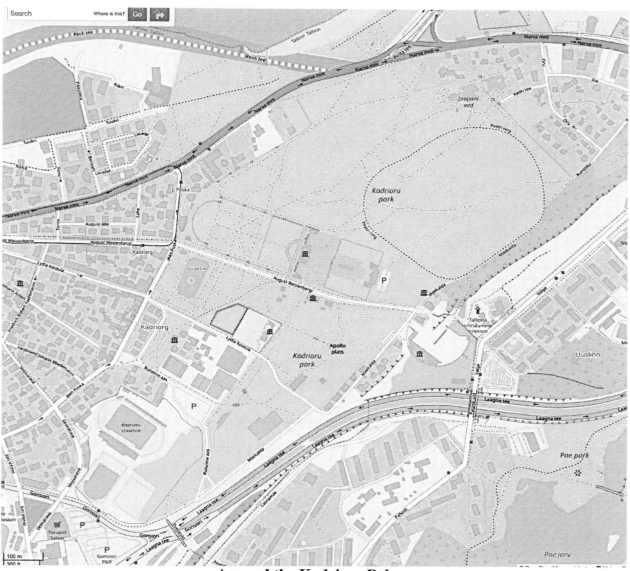

Around the Kadriorg Palace

This map is best viewed directly from OpenStreetMap.com on your personal device where it can be expanded or one specific area can be enlarged. Given the format of this book, it is impossible to display maps with the level of detail you might wish to have while actually out exploring the city. But the OpenStreetMap maps used directly are the tool I always rely upon.

There is a storybook magic to the skyline of Old Town Tallinn

The modern skyline encroaches on Old Town Tallinn

The main gate into Lower Old Town

The flavor of Old Town Tallinn, as seen in its narrow streets.

Church spires rise above Lower Old Town streets

The Lower Old Town main market square

Dance performances are held in the market square

The Kadriorg Palace built by Peter the Great

The modern 21ˢᵗ century side of Tallinn

The leafy green suburb of Nomme

The produce market in Nomme reflects Estonia's summer bounty

The ultra-modern Solaris Shopping Mall in the city's downtown

RIGA, LATVIA

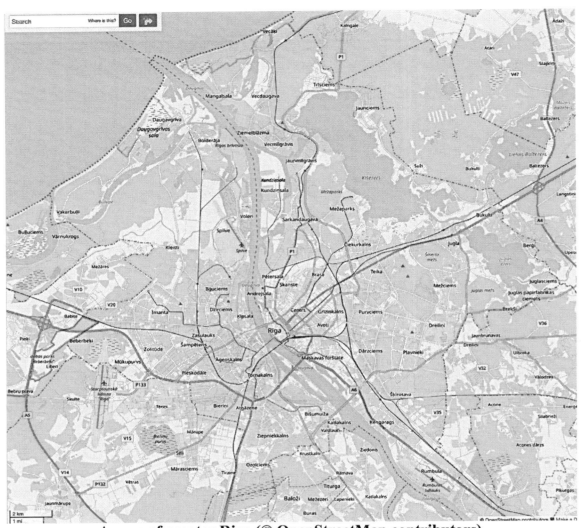

A map of greater Riga (© OpenStreetMap contributors)

Visits to Riga by cruise ships are becoming more frequent. For several years, the Latvian government imposed such high fees for docking that most cruise lines chose to avoid the port. Now the fee schedule is more in line with other Baltic ports and the city of Riga is deriving benefits. Like Tallinn, the city of Riga was also not well known among North American or Western European visitors unless they had ancestry from this region.

At one time Riga was the home to a large Jewish population and many of those Jews migrated to Canada or the United States. Americans or Canadians of Jewish ancestry from Latvia would have been aware of the city's existence. World War II decimated the remaining Jewish population.

Today Riga is becoming better known for its beautiful architecture and parks, and rightly so, as it is the largest city in the three Baltic States with a metropolitan population of 1,018,000, yet it has the feel of a small and unhurried city with very little traffic congestion.

THE NATURAL SETTING: Latvia is the middle of the three states referred to as the Baltic Republics. It occupies 64,589 square kilometers or 24,938 square miles, making it approximately the size of the American state of South Carolina. Estonia lies to the north and Lithuania is situated to the south

The landscape of Latvia is one of lush green countryside, dominated by low hills and flat plains. There are many lakes and marshes of glacial origin. The Baltic Sea indents itself deeply into the country in what is called the Gulf of Riga. Latvia is covered in the same mixed broadleaf deciduous and coniferous forest as Estonia, but much land has been cleared for agriculture over many centuries. There is more fine glacial sediment found in Latvia, providing for a healthy agricultural base

Summers are short, but warm and moist thus enabling limited agricultural production of grains, fruits and vegetables. Being just farther south than Estonia by a about a degree or so of latitude, the country has a slightly longer summer with just about a degree Celsius of more summer warmth. Winters are long and cold with heavy snowfall, but in the last decade winters have tended to be milder, as is true throughout the Baltic region.

A BRIEF LOCAL HISTORY: Latvian prehistory can be traced back to ancient hunting peoples over 9,000 years before the modern calendar. But it was not until the 13th century AD that Germanic armies conquered the country and forced its ways, including Christianity, upon the tribal peoples.

The city of Riga began to develop as a trade center during the early part of the middle ages with strong Viking influences because they found that the Daugava River gave access to the interior and they were interested in spreading their trade network far and wide.

Christianity came to the city by decree when the Pope ordered an armed contingent to land in 1200 to forcibly convert the people. And by 1282, the city of Riga was a member of the Hanseatic League and fully involved in economic interaction with the entire Baltic region. Because of its location, it served as a gateway to the interior of Russia before the establishment of Saint Petersburg in the early 18th century.

Because Riga was an important center in the Hanseatic League, this period accounts for much of the Old Town's architecture. During the period 1558 to 1583, the country fell under combined Lithuanian and Polish Rule, and by 1600 much of the territory came under the control of Sweden. The Swedes brought many schools to the common people and eased the impact of rural serfdom, so to this day it is remembered as a peaceful period in Latvian history.

Because of the split of the country between Swedish and Germanic/Polish influences, the northern part of the country accepted the Lutheran faith while southern Latvia was drawn into the Catholic Church. There was also a large Jewish population in Latvia, which remained an important spiritual and cultural force impacting the entire nation until World War II when most Latvian Jews were decimated during the Holocaust.

During the 18th century, Russia became the dominant political influence and many of the Swedish reforms were erased, leaving the peasants once again under the control of wealthy land barons. Rural freedoms would not be seen again until the 19th century when reforms allowed free farmers to claim pieces of land.

In Riga and the few other cities, industrialization brought about a more enlightened work force whose views were anti tsarist, sparking unrest among the people. This ultimately led to an explosion of nationalism not only in Latvia, but also in the other two Baltic states. It erupted in violence along with the 1905 uprisings within Russia proper and can now be looked at as one of the preludes to the Russian Revolution.

The three Baltic States had a brief period of independence following World War I because of a weakened Germany and Russia's civil war and the start of the Communist Era. This period of independence was short lived. At the start of Nazi hostilities, the Soviet Union infiltrated Latvia in 1940, and incorporated it into their nation. In less than a year, the Germans invaded the Baltic States on their march toward Saint Petersburg, which was at that time known as Leningrad. More than 200,000 Latvians and 70,000 Latvian Jews were exterminated during this period of occupation. After the Soviet Union re took the Baltic region, there were many harsh measures placed upon the people, as part of the overall system of collectivization of agriculture and industry. Thousands were either deported to Siberia or executed. This stands in sharp contrast with the original plan for the Soviet Union in which each ethnic republic was to govern its own internal affairs.

Under Mikhail Gorbachev, a relaxation of restrictions on the Baltic peoples ultimately led to the full independence of each by 1991. And by 1994, all Russian military troops were withdrawn. Like in Estonia, there are those in Latvia who fear that today's Russian nationalism and the outspoken pledges to protect the interests of Russian speakers in bordering states could lead to a possible invasion. Canada has sent a small contingent to demonstrate NATO's concern over the future of the Baltic States since Latvia is a member of NATO as well as the European Union. I personally believe that such perceived military threats are minimized by the umbrella of both the European Union and NATO. These Baltic countries are not the Ukraine where Russia's justification for invasion or infiltration is based upon a past common history dating back centuries.

Like its neighbors to the north and south, Latvia is now an independent parliamentary democracy, a member of the European Union and NATO. And it recently joined the Eurozone. It is enjoying new freedoms and economic prosperity along with a newly found tourist trade given that for so long it was a rather drab and dreary place to visit under the Soviet system. Like Estonia, the Latvian nation became heavily dominated over by the Soviet Union after World War II, with many Russian factory workers having been moved into the country by the Communist government. However, the percentage of Russian descendants is not as high as it is in Estonia and thus there is not as much of a feeling of tension between the two ethnic groups today.

The people of Latvia share many cultural traits in common with the other two Baltic nations, but each is distinct despite the many similarities that they share with one another. The Latvian language is totally unique and is distantly related to the language of Lithuania, its southern neighbor. The cuisine, music and traditional costumes are similar to both of its Baltic neighbors despite the linguistic and cultural differences.

THE PHYSICAL LAYOUT OF THE CITY OF RIGA: Being a small country, the capital city of Riga is the largest city and cultural hearth of the nation. The city is situated along the Daugava River just a few miles inland from the Gulf of Riga. Dredging has made the river navigable to large oceangoing vessels, and Riga is the most important seaport of the three Baltic nations. Since the start of recorded history, the Daugava River valley has been seen as a transit route for merchants and the spreading of cultural ideas between the coast and the interior of west central Russia.

Because of the tide of invaders throughout its history, the city of Riga reflects influences from Poland, Sweden, Germany and Russia in both its architecture and its overall cultural flavor. But because of immigrants from Germany coming to dominate the city's commerce, the German population at one point came to over 40 percent of the city with German being the second language of the streets. However, later Russian domination, especially during the Soviet Era, made Russian the official language in both written and spoken forms. Only now has the Latvian language once again taken center stage as the official language of the country. However, many people still regularly speak Russian and German in their daily activities.

The city of Riga did suffer damage and great loss of life during both World Wars I and II. It is estimated that over 30 percent of the population perished during World War II alone, especially the city's large and important Jewish population. As in Estonia, the Russians forcibly transferred thousands of their own citizens into Latvia to help justify their takeover of the country. Most of these people settled in Riga and many of their descendants remain today, a potential source of friction existing with the Latvian majority.

The main part of the city of Riga is situated on the eastern bank of the Daugava River and it spreads out from the Old Town core. Here the streets encircle the original main square where the House of Blackheads, which is the old Town Hall, exhibits the excesses of Hanseatic design. Across the square is the new town hall, which actually dates to the early 19th century. Old Town was once surrounded by a wall, but today the beautiful Kronvalda Park through which runs a small chain of lakes indicates where the wall once stood backed up by a moat. Within this confine is a collection of buildings dating as far back as the late middle ages lining narrow streets that are mainly pedestrian oriented. But unlike Tallinn, motor vehicles are permitted on many of the streets, and there have been permits issued for the construction of modern buildings.

Beyond the park is the newer city of Riga. The main street of Brivibas Ilea begins at the Kronvalda Park and extends in a straight line northeastward, essentially dividing the new city in half. The central core revolves around this street with essentially regular blocks and extends outward for several kilometers. Other major streets radiate out from Kronvalda Park and the various districts of the city have formed around these major boulevards. In the northern end of the park, along and to the north of Elizabetes Ilea is a late 19th century area of Art Nouveau architecture that has no equal anywhere else in Europe. For those who appreciate this style of architecture the district has become very much of a tourist attraction.

As one gets farther out from the modern city core, there are still many areas that show the rather regularized and non-descript apartment blocks built during the Soviet Era after World War II. These same apartment buildings are seen in almost every city of the former Soviet Union. Today with the economic prosperity in Latvia, many of these buildings are either being modernized or replaced.

Architecturally Riga is more Germanic and Polish in flavor with many large and imposing old churches, palatial homes and a massive castle. Unlike Tallinn, which appears more like a Scandinavian city, Riga tends to bear a stronger physical resemblance to cities in Germany or Poland. The city's Old Town has been declared a World Heritage Site by UNESCO and is today the focus of tourism, just as is true in Tallinn. In the city's central core there are very few modern high-rise buildings. Old Riga developed along the eastern bank of the Daugava River. Its architecture shows the impact of the city having been a major trade center during the 18th and 19th centuries, as unlike Tallinn, the buildings in Riga are more commodious and show a greater degree of affluence. The few medieval buildings that survive, especially the old Town Hall, known as the House of Blackheads, are far more ornate and elegant in style than any seen in the other two Baltic States. The two great cathedrals are also built of brick and stone and present magnificent facades and towers, again displaying the city's great position of influence. The Russian Orthodox Cathedral is late 19th century in origin and built just beyond where the wall of the Old Town once stood, which today is a beautiful crescent shaped park that bounds the Old Town. Unlike Tallinn, the wall that once surrounded the landward side of Riga has long since disappeared, save for a small segment. It is now the park that delineates the Old Town from the modern city center to the north.

West of the Daugava River is the newer part of Riga that has only more recently seen development. The most modern office and residential towers in the city are found lining the western bank of the river and stand in quite a degree of contrast to the church spires of Old Riga on the eastern bank. There is a growing number of very modern high-rise towers being constructed along the west bank of the Daugava River along with some notable pieces of public architecture such as the city's dramatic library. But beyond the riparian zone, the western part of the city consists of distinct small districts some of which are of 19th century vintage with beautiful private homes while others contain the grim apartment blocks of the Soviet period. And still other newer districts represent modern 21st century residential development. They are stitched together by several major boulevards that radiate out from the three major bridges that cross the river. The western bank is difficult for visitors to reach, as it is too far to walk from where cruise ships dock. Local bus or trolley bus service is available, but the Riga tourist offices have not publicized the use of public transport for visitors. Riga still is developing its tourist infrastructure.

There is no Metro and mass transit system of busses and electric trolleys that can be accessed easily. The ships dock very close to the Old Town, enabling visitors who do not go on tour to see the most historic parts of Riga. The best options for getting around on one's own are:

* Taking the ship-sponsored overview tour, which generally involves driving around the city and having the major highlights pointed out while a guide provides narration. There are also ship sponsored walking tours of the Old Town district, providing the narration you do not get on your own.

* Utilizing the hop on hop off bus as both a means of overview, but also to enable you to visit more venues with less walking. And you have the benefit of narration, giving you a better comprehension of the city.

* Your cruise line can arrange a private car and driver/guide, but their charges are often quite high. I would recommend contacting *www.limousine-service.lv* for information regarding private touring availability and prices. This is the largest limousine company in the city.

* Walking is a great option, as cruise ships dock alongside the Old Town and you can explore much of this historic district and into the modern city on foot if you are capable. There are many cafes, bistros and coffee shops where you can have a respite during the day and if the weather is nice, this is a good way to enjoy the historic district. And the Art Nouveau streets are also within walking distance to the northwest of the Old Town.

In my many visits to Riga, I did an overview tour the first time, and in successive visits I have simply concentrated upon walking in one or two areas at a time. But I do have the advantage of visiting on multiple occasions, which most cruise passengers do not have. By combining an overview with your own or a ship-sponsored walking tour, you will be able to come away with a distinct feel for Riga.

My recommendations for the sights to be seen in Riga include the following (listed in alphabetical order):

* Alberta Ilea - Located in the northwest part of the central new city, this street dates to the early 20th century and is lined with an assortment of Art Nouveau apartment blocks. The architecture is quite unique in that so many Art Nouveau

structures are grouped together in one street. The local tourist representative who comes on board ship will show you how to walk to this street not far from the ship's dock. It is also clearly marked on tourist maps. If you go there first from the ship it is only six blocks walk along beautifully shaded streets

* Central Market - Located just east of the Old Town area, this is one of the largest and most elaborate public markets in the Baltic States. The displays of meats, seafood, cheese, breads, condiments, fruits, vegetables and baked goods will make your mouth water. It will also give you a better understanding of Latvian cuisine. The market is open seven days a week from 7 AM to 6 PM, but individual shops or stalls may not adhere to these basic hours.

* House of Blackheads - This is the most iconic building in Riga. The meeting hall was built in 1334, during the height of the Hanseatic League's role in the city, and it is an exceptionally ornate and distinctive building. The original building was bombed during World War II, but has been faithfully reconstructed. It is open from 11 AM to 6 PM daily, but closed on Mondays.

* Jugenda Stila Nami - A collection of distinctive three-dimensional Art Nouveau buildings of the Jugenstil style that is not seen in other cities, this is still another pride of the city. The buildings are located on Elizabetes and Strelnieku Streets, which meets with Alberta Ilea. Any tourist bureau map will show this district. If you are already planning to visit Alberta Ilea, this collection is just a continuation of the Art Nouveau style.

* Kronvalda Park - This large park encircles the landward side of the Old Town. It is beautifully landscaped, has small lakes and fountains along with flower beds to provide an overall quiet green space between the old and new cities. There are beautiful fountains, vibrant flower beds and portions of the former moat that reflect the sky and trees on a bright sunny day. The park is an excellent place to rest, especially on a warm day. It is also a great place to simply people watch. It is also a great place to just relax and enjoy the fresh air.

* Latvian Ethnographic Open Air Museum - Located not too far from the city center, this museum provides a look into the past centuries of Latvian life, especially that of the rural lifestyle. It is located at the far northeastern edge of the city and can be reached easily by taxi. The address is Brīvības gatve 440, Vidzemes priekšpilsēta and it is open from 10 AM to 5 PM daily.

* Museé Art Nouveau - Located on Alberta Ilea, this museum provides those who are devotees of Art Nouveau even more upon which to feast the eyes. The museum is open daily except Monday from 10 AM to 6 PM.

* Museum of the Occupation of Latvia - This is a venue for true history buffs, as it presents in vivid detail the Imperial, Nazi and Soviet occupation of Latvia. It is located at Raiņa bulvāris 7 in the heart of the Old Town. It is open daily from 11 AM to 6 PM. The subject matter is rather disturbing and the museum definitely points to the hardships of the Latvian people during so much of the 20th century.

* **Riga Ghetto and Latvian Holocaust Museum** - This small museum tells the grim story of life in the Riga Ghetto and then of the Nazi occupation of the city and the ultimate extermination of the Jewish population. Unlike visiting holocaust museums in North American or Western European cities, here you are visiting a museum in a city that witnessed the horrors of the genocide. The museum is just south of the Old Town at Maskavas iela 14A, Latgales priekšpilsēta, easily reached by taxi. On foot it is about two miles southeast of where the ship docks along the riverfront. The museum is open daily from 10 AM to 6 PM, but closed on Saturday. This is not a happy place to visit, but for anyone who cares about the history of World War II and the holocaust, it is a must see venue.

* **Rumbula Forest Memorial** - If one of the ship tours does not include this rather grim, yet vital memorial, you can reach it by either a privately reserved car and driver/guide or local taxi. This is a memorial in what is now a peaceful forest clearing. But once Jews were brought here and slaughtered during the Nazi occupation of Riga. This memorial is located on Highway A-6 about 25 miles southeast of the city. It is a very somber site to visit, but it is an important part of learning about the horrors of the holocaust. Visiting is a sobering experience similar to that of one of the concentration camps in Poland, but it is a sobering reminder of the horrors of the Holocaust.

* **Saint Peter's Church** - This is the main Lutheran church for Old Town, and its tower is quite famous for having a viewing platform that can be reached via an old fashioned elevator. The views of the city are most dramatic, especially on a clear day. It is open from 10 AM to 6 PM weekdays and Saturday, but closed Monday. Sunday it is open from Noon until 6 PM.

* **Town Hall Square of Old Town** - Around the main square you will see many examples of the medieval and Hanseatic architecture of Riga. This is the heart of Old Town. Quite often there will be musicians or dancers performing, dressed in traditional costumes.

Some cruise lines will offer journeys out into the countryside for those who want to experience the rural flavor of Latvian life. You can also plan a journey for all or part of the day into the countryside with a private car and driver. The Latvian countryside is very idyllic and peaceful and affords you an opportunity to experience a way of life that seems to still be rooted in the past. But unless you have been to Riga before, you will miss the beautiful architecture and flavor of the city.

If the weather is nice and you want to enjoy the beach, I highly recommend going to the main Riga railway station and taking the short 30-minute train trip to Jūrmala, the popular Riga beach resort on the Gulf of Riga. Jūrmala was once a favored seaside playground for high-ranking Soviet officials who would come from as far away as Moscow. There are many fine examples of wood 18th and 19th century architecture plus a few reminders of the rather boxy Soviet style used for public buildings such as hotels. The beach at Jūrmala is composed of a beautiful white quartz sand that sparkles in the summer sun. And the beach extends as a thin strand for over 20 miles, backed up by marshes and woodland. Once again I only recommend this option if you have already been to Riga on a previous trip.

LATVIAN CUISINE: For those who enjoy experiencing the food culture of a country, the Public Market at the south end of the Old Town is highly recommended. Here you will find displays of the produce, meats, seafood, cheese, breads and other delicacies in the Latvian diet. If you wish to do more than sample the cuisine, there are many restaurants located in the Old Town area. I have not expanded my horizon, so I have a few that I recommend. They are typically Latvian and are quite excellent:

* Aleks Restaurant - This is definitely not a restaurant that you would find on most lists for visitors. This is a small restaurant attached to an equally small hotel on aside street where you can savor the local architecture. The menu offers a variety of local dishes including appetizers, soups entrees and desserts. The quality and freshness are outstanding and the service is very gracious, but not at all pretentious. The address is 24 Jauniela and the restaurant is open from Noon to 10 PM. You will need to have one of the local reps on board the ship mark this obscure location on one of the maps of the old city area of Riga.

* Bar & Restaurant Petergailis – In the heart of Old Town at Skarmu Ilea # 25, this is a beautiful and engaging traditional restaurant serving a wide variety of Latvian and other Eastern European dishes. The cuisine, service and atmosphere are all at a high standard that is sure to please. This is a rather small and somewhat eclectic restaurant so it is best to have the ship's concierge make a booking even for lunch since the restaurant has a good local following. The restaurant is open daily from 10 AM to 11:30 PM.

* Folklubs Ala Pagrabs – Located in the Old Town at Peldu # 19, this very traditional restaurant has very high standards of cuisine and service. The atmosphere is cozy and charming. The menu is diverse and offers many selections among seafood, meat and poultry entrees with all of the traditional accompaniments. Desserts are also quite delicious, so save room. Their hours of service are open from Noon to Monday and Tuesday, staying open to 3 AM Wednesday and 4 AM Thursday and Friday. Saturday and Sunday they are only open between 2 PM and 4 AM. Clearly they have a nighttime following.

* Lido at Atputas Center - Just southeast of the city center along the Daugava River, this recreation center hosts wedding parties and special events as well as having several restaurant choices from sit down menu service to buffet. There is a beer cellar, children's playground, small lake and an overall atmosphere conducive to enjoying an afternoon or evening. The cuisine is a combination of Latvian and Eastern European fare, and the quality is excellent. This is the largest of three Lido restaurants in Riga, and worth the drive out of the city center, but you do need a car and driver/guide, as a taxi there and back would cost just as much and not give you the flexibility of your own vehicle. It is located along Krasta Iela 76. The hours are from 11 AM to 11 PM seven days per week.

* **Lido Old City** - There is also a small Lido Restaurant in the old city located on Tirgonu Iela 6 open from 11 AM to 10 PM, but it is small and often very crowded. I recommend going late for lunch at around 2 or 3 PM to avoid the lunch crowd.

* **Milda** – Located in the heart of the Old Town at Kungu Ilea # 8, this is a very traditional Latvian and Eastern European restaurant with a refined and elegant atmosphere. The cuisine is very traditional and the menu is quite varied with offerings in seafood, meat and poultry and a wide array of side dishes. The restaurant is open Tuesday thru Saturday from Noon to 11 PM and Sunday from Noon to 10 PM.

* **Riits** – This fine restaurant is located beyond the confines of the Old Town, about four blocks east of the Freedom Monument in the city's central district, but easy walking from the ship. The address is Dzirnavu Ilea # 72 and should not be hard to find. You may wish to have the local tourist representative mark it on a city map. The atmosphere is casual and the vibe is that of being out in the Latvian countryside. The cuisine is traditional and well prepared. The menu includes a variety of grilled meats, poultry and fresh seafood. They have a wide variety of starters, soups and salads prior to their entrees, most of them grilled over natural oak charcoal. And they are open Monday from Noon to 11 PM and Tuesday thru Sunday from 9 AM to 11 PM.

SHOPPING: There are literally hundreds of small souvenir and craft shops located in the Old Town area of Riga, but I cannot recommend one or the other because I have never patronized any of them. Latvian crafts include embroidery, dolls and many household items, but I would be reluctant to speak to quality or artistry. For regular shopping, there is a Stockmann Department Store located in the new city center on Satekles Iela. It is part of a large center that also contains one of the city's major cinemas.

I realize that my information regarding shopping is limited to just the major department store, but I do not wish to provide information I have not personally verified.

A FINAL NOTE: Riga is a city that is just now starting to become more of a household word among people who have cruised the Baltic Sea. As more cruise lines include this beautiful city on their itinerary, Riga may become as well-known as Tallinn. The architecture, parks and friendly people will win over visitors and this will help to spread the word about visiting Riga. For anyone who had family living in Latvia during World War II, there is a strong interest in seeing the city that for many will hold sad memories, thus making the visit somewhat of a pilgrimage. This would also hold true for anyone who is a direct descendant of those who escaped the years under Soviet domination.

RIGA MAPS

THE CENTRAL CITY

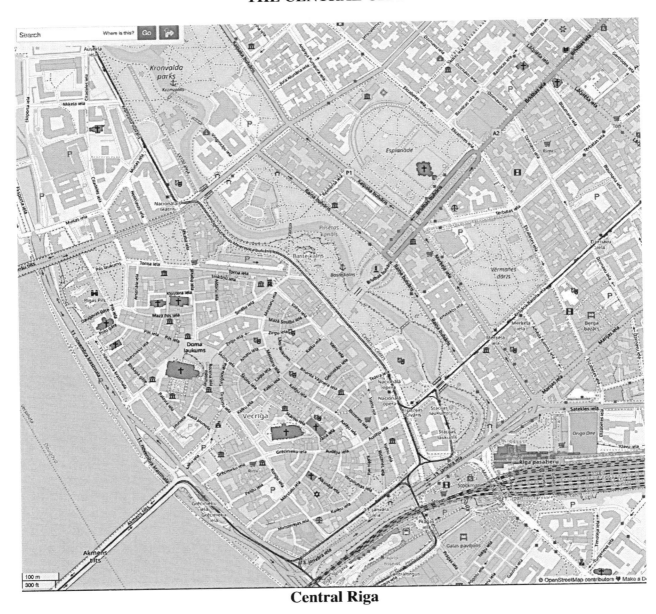

Central Riga

This map is best viewed directly from OpenStreetMap.com on your personal device where it can be expanded or one specific area can be enlarged. Given the format of this book, it is impossible to display maps with the level of detail you might wish to have while actually out exploring the city. But the OpenStreetMap maps used directly are the tool I always rely upon.

THE RIGA OLD TOWN

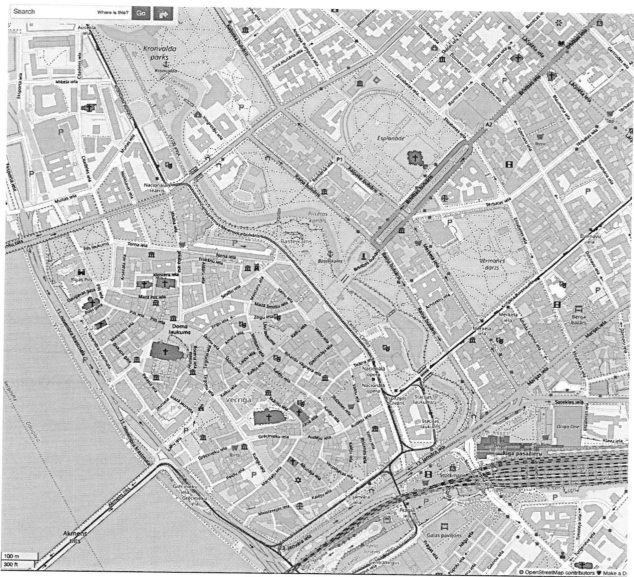

The Old Town area

This map is best viewed directly from OpenStreetMap.com on your personal device where it can be expanded or one specific area can be enlarged. Given the format of this book, it is impossible to display maps with the level of detail you might wish to have while actually out exploring the city. But the OpenStreetMap maps used directly are the tool I always rely upon.

THE ART NOUVEAU AND DOWNTOWN AREAS

Art Nouveau (upper left) and downtown Riga

This map is best viewed directly from OpenStreetMap.com on your personal device where it can be expanded or one specific area can be enlarged. Given the format of this book, it is impossible to display maps with the level of detail you might wish to have while actually out exploring the city. But the OpenStreetMap maps used directly are the tool I always rely upon.

A view over the heart of the city of Riga from the Radisson Hotel

The new Riga skyline on the west side of the Daugava River

There are many new high rises on the west side of the Daugava River

Old Town streets are lined with small cafes

The Riga Castle in Old Town

The gingerbread charm of Old Town Riga

The Riga Dom, one of three major Old Town churches

An example of Art Nouveau architecture on Alberta Iela

Flower gardens outside of the Riga Opera House

Beautiful Kronvalda Park where once the city moat existed

Kronvalda Park around the Old Town where the wall once stood is very tranquil

The Latvian Freedom Monument

Melerovica Boulevard in the modern city

Great variety of foods in the Central Market

Baltic amber is one item visitors are always looking to buy

KLAIPÉDA, LITHUANIA

A map of greater Klaipéda (© OpenStreetMap contributors)

The majority of cruise itineraries, especially for the large mega ships, do not include a stop in Klaipéda, Lithuania. I believe the main reason that Lithuania is avoided is because of the nature of the population distribution. The main center of population and cultural activity is in the far eastern corner of the country, too far from the Baltic Sea coast for access during a one-day port call. Even though this is also true for Poland and Germany, the conditions are different. In Poland the port cities of Gdańsk and Gdynia combined have over 1,000,000 residents and are historically very significant. In Germany the port cities of Warnemunde and Rostock combined have nearly 400,000 residents and are rich in history. And in addition, Berlin is easily accessible during the long one-day port call made by all cruise lines.

THE NATURAL SETTING: Klaipéda is the only seaport for the nation of Lithuania. Unlike Estonia or Latvia, Lithuania is not blessed with a seacoast that is amenable to trade. The long sand bar, known as the Curonian Spit, blocks most of the coastline from direct access. The bay inside this bar is very shallow and needs to be dredged for ships to be able to enter the mouth and reach Klaipéda. Thus although it is a Baltic Sea nation, Lithuania has turned more inland as evidenced by the fact that its capital and largest city of Vilnius is located closer to the border of Belarus than it is to the sea. And when ships dock in Klaipéda it is normally for eight hours or less, thus not providing time for a visit to Vilnius, as road and rail routes are not designed for high-speed travel.

Lithuania is the largest of the three Baltic Sea states with 65,298 square kilometers or 25,212 square miles, making it just slightly larger than Latvia. It only has a population of 3,600,000 people. Its population matrix is such that the Lithuanian people comprise over 80 percent of the total, with the remainder being from surrounding countries, including 8 percent being of Russian origin, far less than in Latvia or Estonia.

Most of the land in Lithuania is rather low in elevation, slightly hilly to flat, again showing the result of glacial action during the ice age. There are over 3,000 lakes that dot the countryside, which in its natural state is a mix of broadleaf and needle leaf woodlands. Unlike its other neighbors, the coastline of Lithuania has few natural harbors, most of it containing marshes and sand dunes, but this unique landscape is quite scenic, a potential now becoming realized. Sand dunes are found scattered around the Baltic Sea, but along the Lithuanian coast, the combination of ocean currents and winds worked together to create a long, narrow sand bar along what was a shallow coastline. Today the Curonian Spit is both a Lithuanian National Park and a UNESCO World Heritage Site, attracting more visitors each year, as word of its existence becomes more widely disseminated.

Winter is once again the dominant season, but being farther south it is not quite as severe as in Estonia or Latvia. This is still a relatively poor nation with regard to resources, one in which agriculture is an important part of the economy. Dairy farming and the raising of pigs and cattle are important. Industries are somewhat developed with shipbuilding and food processing being key to the country's trade balance. Lithuania relies heavily upon trade with Russia from where it obtains most of its raw materials.

A BRIEF LOCAL HISTORY: Lithuania is an old nation, having developed as an amalgamation of semi-nomadic Baltic tribes dating back before our modern calendar. Linguistically the Lithuanian and Latvian people are similar, forming a distinct grouping among Indo European speakers, yet each language is totally unique. Culturally speaking, the Lithuanian people have been heavily influenced by Germans, Poles and Russians and their culture exhibits traits that are a fusion of the three major traditions.

The earliest evidence of a Lithuanian state comes from the 9th century. By 1250, the country was united with Belarus into the Grand Principality of Lithuania. By 1341, the Grand Duke Gediminas had expanded the empire as far south as Kiev, and his dynasty ruled until 1572. Initially a pagan state, the Lithuanians fought off German

Teutonic Knights with an intense ferocity. But eventually the Lithuanians accepted the Catholic faith, which today accounts for 90 percent of the people.

In 1569, Lithuania united with Poland as a commonwealth with each nation having its respective leaders and identity. At its peak, its dominion extended from the Baltic to the Black Sea. During the years from 1772 to 1792, Lithuania disappeared from the map, its vast holdings divided between Prussia, Austria and Russia. What we recognize today as Lithuania was totally absorbed into Russia and the Tsar even was given the title as Grand Prince of Lithuania.

Being a neighbor of German East Prussia brought Lithuania under total control of Germany at the start of World War I. At the end of the war, the Lithuanians declared their independence as a republic, as did Latvia and Estonia. In 1940, the Soviet Union invaded Lithuania and absorbed it as a Soviet Socialist Republic. But when Nazi Germany attacked Russia in 1941, Lithuania came under Nazi control. It was not liberated until 1945, but it was then reabsorbed into the Soviet Union. It was not until the Soviet state collapsed at the end of 1990 that Lithuania finally once again emerged as an independent republic. The country joined the European Union in 2004 along with Estonia. The Euro became the official currency at the start of 2015, replacing the short-lived Litu, which had been the currency since 1991.

THE PHYSICAL LAYOUT OF THE CITY OF KLAIPÉDA: Klaipéda is not physically very large, and the Dané River splits the city in half. The street pattern is surprisingly regular with all major streets oriented on a north to south and east to west axis. North of the Dané River is the city center, which has a strong Soviet Era architecture with the exception of two dominant high-rise towers. The central core is relatively small and many of the buildings house both shops on lower floors and apartments above. There is a lack of any feeling of being in a major city. There are few shops and no major stores in the central core. It is as much residential as it is commercial.

The small Old Town area is located south of the Dané River, but even here the streets form essentially rectangular blocks. But this area of about half a square kilometer has many buildings that date back to the 17th and 18th centuries and most of the streets are cobbled. Klaipéda has been restoring its Old Town, the core area of the city that features cobblestone streets, antique lampposts and old buildings that represent centuries of history. Many of the old buildings exhibit what is called "fachwork," timber-framed architecture, a style seen in German coastal communities. There are no monumental churches, palaces or other buildings of significance.

Beyond the Old Town, the architectural flavor is Soviet Era in nature with large apartment blocks and few single-family houses until you reach the outer edge of the city. But there are a few quite tall and modern apartment blocks in this area that reflect the growing prosperity in the post-Soviet period.

Around the mouth of the Dané River is the port area, which occupies both the north and south shores. The port is not very large, but it does handle all of the country's import and export traffic that is done by sea. There are also small shipbuilding and repair facilities.

Opposite the port, across the water is the Curonian Spit and facing the city are some rather elegant homes that can only be reached by ferryboat. Most of the spit is either cloaked in scrubby pine forest or stands as raw sand dunes. It is this natural landscape that has attracted campers, hikers and beachgoers in recent years. And its unusual character is what has given it both national park status by the Lithuanian government and UNESCO World Heritage Status.

BRIEF COMMUNITY HISTORY: Klaipéda is Lithuania's third city in population, but its primary port, dating back to its origination in 1252. There is a strong feeling of being in Germany when one looks at the architecture of Klaipéda, and German is the most commonly spoken language apart from native Lithuanian.

The original name of the town was Memel, a truly Germanic name. During the 17th century, the Swedes devastated the city, and later during the 18th century, the Russians occupied it for a five-year period. In the early 19th century, Klaipéda became the temporary capital of Prussia when Napoleonic forces occupied Berlin. Throughout its history, this city has been tied closely to, if not a part of the German state.

In the late 19th century, this northern part of Prussia was turned into an international zone, occupied by French troops, but in 1923, the new nation of Lithuania forced the French out and incorporated it into their own country. Klaipéda gives one more the flavor of Germany than they would have traveling inland to Vilnius, the national capital and the true core city of Lithuanian culture.

During World War II, Klaipéda served as a major submarine port for the German Navy, thus it came under attack from allied forces, being liberated by the Red Army in 1945, but at the expense of severe devastation. After the war, Lithuania, like its neighbors Latvia and Estonia, was absorbed into the Soviet Union where it remained as a Soviet Socialist Republic until 1991, the Russians claiming that the territory had once been theirs. Although the Soviet system brought industrial infrastructure, it also kept the people from expressing their own cultural traditions.

Today Klaipéda is undergoing a major revitalization. Lithuania is now a member of the European Union, and with the country's heartland located to the interior around the capital city of Vilnius; Klaipéda is the country's gateway to the sea. The city is also home to a major fishing fleet, and it is considered to be the most important fishing port on the entire Baltic Sea. A major maritime museum, housed in an old German fort on the Neringa Peninsula, now depicts the marine life and maritime heritage of the region.

Lithuania's coastline offers few good anchorages, but here between the Dané River and the Curonian Lagoon, the city was able to cater to ships bringing trade goods and carrying away the country's exports. The city is separated from the open sea by a narrow sandy spit, facing the shallow inside lagoon that needed to be dredged to deepen it for major cruise vessels. The sand spit known as the Kursiu Nerija is today a national park, preserving the sandy dunes and thick woodlands. This is also a recreational area that is far more rural than urban. As ships sail into Klaipéda, the pass along the inside edge of this natural parkland, having the city itself on the port (left) side. The entire Lithuanian coastline is hidden behind this barrier, thus offering little access to the sea for trade.

Before World War II, Klaipéda had a thriving Jewish population that amounted to over 17 percent of the city's population. Most either fled the city prior to German occupation, and the remainder along with the rest of Lithuania's 235,000 Jews, were exterminated in Nazi concentration camps. Today only a handful of Jews live in Klaipéda, but the city does maintain one small synagogue, a reminder of its past history.

SIGHTSEEING FEATURES: Of the few monuments in Klaipéda, most were desecrated by the Soviets when they re took the city from Nazi control in the later years of World War II, and then continued their degradation of Lithuanian culture during the occupation that lasted until 1991. Those seen today are actually reconstructions of older works, based upon old photographs. The city's old Theatre Square houses a neoclassical theatre, but this is a reproduction of the original structure, which burned in a fire during the 19th century. Southeast of the square, the History Museum of Lithuania is a venue that offers many of the typical costumes and artifacts of the region.

Many cruise lines offer just brief sightseeing tours of Klaipéda by either motor coach or as a walking visit. But if you are staying in town, it is so easy to get around on your own. All you will miss is the narration, but with my book or any other major tourist guide, you will have all you need to know. Some of the more upscale cruise lines will offer a half or full day tour out into the Lithuanian countryside, which is a nice opportunity to get away from the port.

Klaipéda is too small to have any hop on hop off bus service. And it does not receive that many cruise visitors per summer season to warrant such service.

You can request a car and driver/guide through your cruise line, or you can contact JND for information, fees and bookings at *www.jnd.lt* They offer both self-drive vehicles and driver/guides as well.

The few sights worthy of special note are listed below, and are generally included on any ship tours of the city, or can be accessed on your own if you choose to visit privately (shown in alphabetical order):

* Drama Theater - Facing the Dramatic Theater Square, the theater was initially developed in 1935, under strong German influence. It is a beautiful building, but tours are not given. Unless there is a daytime performance when your ship is in port, there is no way to view the interior. If there happens to be a performance during the afternoon of your visit, you can attend providing tickets are available. It would be rare, however, for any performance to be held in English.

* Dramatic Theater Square - Generally when a ship is in port, local craftspeople and artists will set up their wares around the Annchen Tharau Fountain adjacent to the city's small dramatic theater. Some of the craft items or art work pieces are quite good even though they are the work of amateurs. Over the years I have purchased a beautiful hand embroidered tablecloth and two small oil paintings at very reasonable prices. And as an art collector, I consider the work to be quite excellent.

* Klaipéda Old Town - You can walk the entire Old Town in less than 30 minutes. The architecture is far from monumental, but it does give you a good look at what life was like in this once primarily Germanic city. At the south end of Old Town is an open air public market, but it is not very large.

* Kursiu Nerija National Park - Located across the lagoon on the Curonian Spit, this is the most important tourist attraction in Klaipéda. Tours are offered in either all-terrain vehicles or by bicycle for those who want to enjoy a taste of this natural landscape, which is unique to the Baltic Sea area. A local ferry operates across the lagoon on a regular basis from adjacent to the cruise dock. But without renting a bicycle or participating in a local all-terrain tour, the most you can do is take a short walk through the woods and dunes to the open seaside.

* Lithuanian Clock and Watch Museum - This is a rather strange small museum, as it is devoted to timepieces. I would only recommend it to those who have a specific interest in the subject. It is located in the city center at Liepu g. #6. It is open Monday thru Saturday from Noon to 6 PM.

* Martynas Mazvydas Sculpture Park - A short walk east of the city center, this small, but well-manicured park is home to around 100 sculptures, but of contemporary origin. The oldest of the sculptures only dates to the 1980's, but it is still a nice way to spend half an hour taking in the work of Lithuanian sculptors. Being located along the river starting at the second bridge and running for two blocks, it is always open.

SHOPPING: There are a few arts and crafts shops in the Old Town, but I have found their prices to be higher and the quality no better than that found in the square. Over the years I have purchased two oil paintings, as noted above, that represent the work of highly talented, but from unknown artists in the square. The quality of the work is outstanding. So I advise you check the marketplace in the square prior to spending money in one of the shops. You may make a great find at far less expense.

CUISINE: Lithuanian cuisine is strongly influenced by Russian and Polish traditions, which means lots of cabbage, potatoes and beets, with pork being the most popular meat. For lunch during summer a cold, creamy beet soup served with cold boiled potato or hard-boiled egg is a popular dish, and is essentially very Russian or Polish. The national dish is called "Zeppelin," named for the large German airships. It is an elongated potato dough stuffed with meat or cheese and then baked or fried. It is covered with crumbled bacon. The Lithuanians brew up a Czech style lager that is considered to be very good. Also there are a few local wines available.

There are several small restaurants in Klaipéda. Most of the restaurants are quite casual, but there are a couple in my listing that are more upmarket. As a small city with a limited number of outside visitors, it is hard to find a large array of quality restaurants. I have listed what I consider to be the best:

* Momo Grill - Located in the newer city north of the Dané River at Liepu Str. 20 and open from 11 AM to 10 PM, this is also an outstanding rather elegant restaurant. It is very small and only has less than ten tables, but the food and service are surprisingly quite excellent.

* Monai – At Liepu G # 4 in the city center, this traditional restaurant features Lithuanian dishes along with many representing other cultures of Eastern Europe. They also serve vegetarian entrees as well. The entrees are beautifully prepared and served in a warm and friendly atmosphere. Their hours are from 11:30 AM to 10 PM Tuesday thru Friday, Saturday from 11 AM to 10 PM and Sunday from 11 AM to 4 PM.

* Stora Antis - A small, upmarket restaurant and hotel. It serves traditional cuisine with much care as to freshness and flavors. The location is south of the Dané River at Tiltų g. #6. It is only open for dinner from 5 to 11 PM Tuesday thru Saturday, which is only going to work if your ship is staying into the mid evening hours.

* Taverna Ferdinandis – Just to the north of the main city center and close to the harbor at Naujoi G # 10, this restaurant features a broad range of Eastern European menu items with more of an emphasis upon Russian cuisine. But it does not ignore its home Lithuanian roots. I found the cuisine to be superb and the service friendly. But I did notice on Trip Advisor that a couple of people wrote rather stinging reviews while the vast majority wrote five-star reviews. I guess you cannot please everyone, but I did want you to take note of this. I personally found it to be especially good. The restaurant is open Monday thru Friday from 10 AM to Midnight, Saturday Noon to Midnight and Sunday Noon to 6 PM.

SHOPPING: If the artists have set up their wares in the square outside of the Dramatic Theater, those of you interested in local crafts may find some treasures. Lithuanian women are known for their embroidery, generally on linen. Tablecloths or runners are often available at very reasonable prices for hand-made work. There are a few local landscape artists that have not been discovered. They are older men and women who either paint as a hobby or to supplement their retirement. But the work is moderately good, and you can buy a miniature oil painting of acceptable quality for around €20 or a larger 10 x 14 inch oil for €40.

FINAL WORDS: Klaipéda offers just a glimpse into Lithuanian culture, especially due to the fact that this city has a decidedly more German heritage. But its prosperity reflects the rapid growth of the overall nation now that Lithuania has become a member of the European Union. Many cruise guests often ask why the ship stopped here for the day, not realizing that even though this is not an exciting port of call, it does offer a somewhat rare opportunity to visit a country that is not on most traveler's agendas.

Clearly Lithuania is on track to become an important trading partner within the European Union. The national economy is expanding at a healthy rate, and the city of Klaipéda accounts for a share of that expansion. Once the highway infrastructure of Lithuania reaches the standard of its Scandinavian neighbors with the development of more divided expressways, it would become possible for cruise ship passengers to visit Vilnius when ships dock for the day in Klaipéda, just as it is possible to visit Warsaw or Berlin from Baltic Sea ports when ships dock

KLAIPÉDA MAPS

THE CITY OF KLAIPÈDA

The city of Klaipéda

This map is best viewed directly from OpenStreetMap.com on your personal device where it can be expanded or one specific area can be enlarged. Given the format of this book, it is impossible to display maps with the level of detail you might wish to have while actually out exploring the city. But the OpenStreetMap maps used directly are the tool I always rely upon.

THE HEART OF KLAIPÉDA

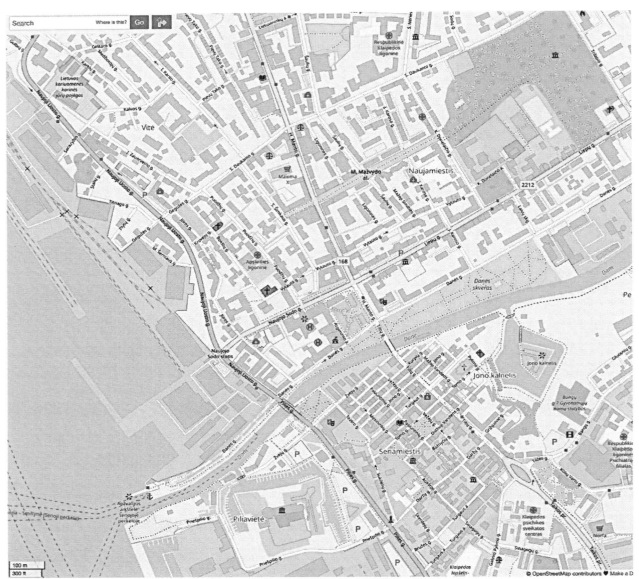

The commercial core of Klaipéda

This map is best viewed directly from OpenStreetMap.com on your personal device where it can be expanded or one specific area can be enlarged. Given the format of this book, it is impossible to display maps with the level of detail you might wish to have while actually out exploring the city. But the OpenStreetMap maps used directly are the tool I always rely upon.

131

The northern end of the Curonian Spit entering Klaipéda

The woodlands of the Curonian Spit seen from the lagoon

The central city skyline of Klaipéda from the ship's deck

The modern skyline of Klaipéda

In the park along the north shore of the Dané River

In the park along the south shore of the Dané River

The Dramatic Theater with a few artists selling their wares outside

On the streets of the historic Old Town

Maintaining the Old Town cobbled streets

Typical Soviet Era housing in Klaipéda

A mix of housing and outdoor dining in the city center

Lithuanian musicians often serenade arriving ships

GDAŃSK, POLAND

A map of greater Gdańsk (© OpenStreetMap contributors)

The coast of Poland is home to one of the larger Baltic Sea urban centers - the city of Gdańsk. It is today the center of a metropolitan region of over 1,000,000 people and a major industrial center as well as the most important port for Poland. Many Baltic Sea itineraries include Gdańsk, with the large mega cruise ships docking in Gdynia, as it has better facilities to accommodate them while the smaller cruise liners can dock in the main harbor of Gdańsk. Gdynia is part of the overall metropolitan region of Gdańsk.

THE NATURAL SETTING: Poland is one of the largest and most important nations to share its coastline with the Baltic Sea. But despite the economic and political significance of modern-day Poland, the country's history has been one of here today, gone tomorrow. Throughout the history of Europe, Poland has appeared on the map for a period of time, only to later be carved up by its more aggressive neighbors, Germany to the west, the former Austro-Hungarian Empire to the south and the Russian Empire to the east. But in spite of its absorption into its giant neighbors, the Polish spirit and culture have lived on, a tribute to the will of her people. There is an old expression among the Polish people that is very meaningful - "There will always be a Poland!"

Poland occupies 312,601 square kilometers or 120,696 square miles, approximately the size of the American state of New Mexico. Its shape is roughly oval. From the Baltic Sea on the north, Poland stretches south to the margins of the Carpathian Mountains where it shares a border with the Czech Republic and Slovakia. To the east and west, the borders are open, as most of Poland is flat to gently rolling land. Thus its history of invasions from both east and west is one that gave the Polish people little comfort. The land has exceptionally good fertility, as it is part of the North European Plain, a region of glacial till not unlike the country around the North American Great Lakes. Many rivers drain out of the Carpathian Mountains, all flowing north. The Odra River forms the border with Germany while the Vistula drains through the heart of the country. The capital city of Warsaw is located on the Vistula, and Gdańsk is situated adjacent to its delta. The natural vegetation cover is one of beautiful broadleaf forests, but to the south there are evergreen woodlands, as the land rises into the Carpathian Mountains. Essentially Poland is lush, green and very attractive. It is also quite productive despite the moderately cold winters. Poland has always been able to feed itself, and today that is important with a population of nearly 40,000,000 people. The country has also been blessed with a variety of minerals and deposits of coal in the southwest, thus giving rise to heavy industry and manufacturing. Essentially Poland is both an agricultural and industrial giant among European nations.

Being farther south than the Scandinavian countries, Poland has longer and warmer summers, adding to the productivity of its agriculture. One might expect the winters to be milder, but being farther inland from the moderating influence of the Atlantic Ocean, Poland's winters have been historically long and cold with heavy quantities of snowfall. Today they are slightly more moderate, as is true for much of northern Europe with the impact of climatic change.

A BRIEF LOCAL HISTORY: The Polish people have a great spirit in spite of the many hardships the nation has endured as a result of outside invasion and occupation. But unlike the more somber Russian personality, Polish people have a decidedly more cheerful outlook. The people are outgoing, gregarious and welcoming. This is also a very religious nation, with 95 percent of the population being rather devout Roman Catholic. The late Pope John Paul II came from southern Poland, a source of pride to the citizens of the country even now after his passing. Prior to World War II, Poland also had the largest Jewish population in Europe, but as a result of the Holocaust, that population has been reduced to a mere handful, primarily in the cities of Warsaw and Kraków.

It is important to understand the essentials of Polish history, because the city of Gdańsk has played a pivotal role in the 20th century drama of Poland's independence and that of the rest of the former Soviet bloc of nations formed after World War II. You will be visiting a city that has gone from a German to a Polish persona in less than the last 100 years. But today it is decidedly Polish.

The people of Poland are of Slavic origin, related closely to the Russians, but descendants of western tribes that settled the region around the 6th century. History shows a Polish Principality having been established in 966, turning into the Polish Kingdom in 1024. There is a period of disunity when Poland broke into small principalities from 1138 until it was reunited into one kingdom in 1320. Poland and Lithuania were united in 1569 and their combined power spread as far south as the Black Sea, but between 1772 and 1792. Prussia, Austria and Russia ultimately carved up the united commonwealth, taking both countries off of the map.

During the Napoleonic Wars, the French used Polish soil as a staging ground for their invasion of Russia. The Duchy of Warsaw was established in 1807, essentially as a puppet state to France. But in the Treaty of Vienna in 1815, the Russian held portions of Poland became the Polish Kingdom, but subordinate to the Russian Tsar. Southern Poland, known as Galicia remained within the Austro-Hungarian Empire, but Kraków held on to its status as an independent republic until 1848. The western part of what is modern Poland remained a part of the Prussian Kingdom, which later became Germany.

During World War I, Poland was occupied by German troops, but in 1918, after the collapse of the German war machine, and with Russia in turmoil, Poland declared itself an independent republic. However, that status would not last for very long, and that has been the fate of Poland since its first inception. But it is important to note that despite the changes in political domination, the Polish people have culturally and spiritually always been one. Remember that saying that translates to, "There will always be a Poland!" The critical issues in the Treaty of Versailles, which ended World War I, were how to draw the borders of Germany and East Prussia, hopefully giving Poland more access to the Baltic Sea. Poland received more territory to the west at the expense of Germany, but in the east, most of East Prussia went to the Russians, and the southeastern border with the Ukraine (then a part of Russia) was not drawn favorably to the Poles. In 1920, the Poles united with rebellious Ukrainians in attempting to wrest that region away from Russia while she was engaged in her civil war. The Russians were defeated and in the Treaty of Riga in 1921, Poland was able to annex more territory along its eastern frontier.

Gdańsk, which had long been a part of Prussia and known as Danzig, was designated as a free city administered by the League of Nations but with its external affairs handled by Poland. A Polish military garrison was established and Poland was guaranteed free use of the harbor since the nation had essentially been landlocked. A small corridor of land had been given directly to Poland, cutting off Eastern Prussia physically from Germany. Here the Poles created their own port city of Gdynia, which today is part of the greater Gdańsk region. By 1933, the Nazi Party had gained control of the city administration since a majority of the residents were German and supported the new regime in Germany. And they agitated to have the city returned to German control.

In early 1939, Germany and the Soviet Union negotiated the Ribbentrop-Molotov non-aggression pact in which both powers secretly agreed to divide Poland between them. On September 1, 1939, German gunboats opened fire on the port of Gdańsk, which was nominally controlled by Poland under false pretext that Polish border guards had fired into Germany the day before. Germany also had contended that free access through the Polish Corridor to Gdańsk was vital to the maintenance of East Prussia. World War II essentially began that day, as France and the United Kingdom had pledged to aid Poland in the event of German military action. Thus it can be said that the opening shots of World War II began in Gdańsk and some ship tours will actually take visitors to the exact spot that was fired upon in September 1939.

The German invasion was swift and brutal, a blitzkrieg type of war that did not enable the Poles to even mount a counter offensive. At the same time, the Red Army advanced from the east. The Polish government fled to Paris and later to London while an underground resistance movement attempted to work from within. In the spring of 1941, Germany advanced across the rest of Poland and began its full invasion of Russia, which then put all of Poland under Nazi control.

The war was brutal for Poland. The Germans had considered the Poles along with the Russians as "unter menschen," meaning second class or sub human. As for the Jews and Gypsies, they were not even considered worthy of survival. Massive roundups took place, first herding them into ghetto areas, and ultimately into extermination camps. Among the more than 6,000,000 Jews eliminated by the Nazi, more than half were Polish. Some of the most notorious concentration camps such as Auschwitz and Treblinka were located on Polish soil. Today only about 10,000 Jews remain in Poland, primarily in the two major cities of Warsaw and Kraków. But today among Poles there is a strong identification with Jewish culture. Each year in Warsaw there is a Jewish music festival but the vast majority of participants and attendees are non-Jews.

During the war, over 400,000 Poles fought with the Red Army and an estimated 200,000 fought with western forces. However, when German forces announced in 1943 that they found mass graves of murdered Polish military officers, the Soviet Union broke off relations with the Polish government in exile. One year later, the Red Army marched into Poland on its way to Berlin. This spelled the end of Polish freedom, as the Soviets install a puppet Communist government that for decades would answer to Moscow.

The war saw the death of more than 6,000,000 Poles, including the 3,000,000 Jews plus another 2,500,000 Poles deported to Germany as slave labor. Many of those deported never lived to return to Poland. Of all the countries that suffered during World War II, for its size and population, Poland suffered the most. And then it lost its freedom, as it became a satellite of the Soviet Union. But all during the Cold War period, the Catholic Church defied the Polish Communist government, keeping the faith alive. When Pope John Paul II was elected in 1979, it was a strong message for Communism, and he did his utmost to keep that message of hope alive. The Pope worked tirelessly to keep the Communist government in check and this enabled the practice of religion to a greater degree than in other satellite countries.

The war also brought changes to the map, as Poland was essentially pushed westward by almost 160 kilometers or 100 miles. The Poles lost territory in the east, but the Odra River became its western border, putting Poland's western frontier within only 120 kilometers or 75 miles of Berlin. The Germans living in this corridor were forced to flee, as Poles were given farms and villages at the expense of their former German residents. Where once Gdańsk sat close to the border of Germany and East Prussia on both sides, Poland now ended up with an extensive coastline on the Baltic Sea, placing Gdańsk somewhere in the middle. The land that is now Poland was previously part of Germany. Many older Germans still feel a degree of resentment toward Poland for the loss of the territory.

The Polish people never fully supported the Communist Party, and there were periods of violence when workers went on strike, and of course the Church gave tacit support. The government could not crush worker strikes because of the power of the Church, as was done in other Eastern bloc nations. In 1980, shipyard workers in Gdańsk went on strike and this was the start of the Solidarity labor movement. The strength of the worker's movement led by Lech Walesa caused the government to declare martial law, and it was careful not to ask the Soviet Union for troops. Most of Solidarity's leaders were arrested, but by 1985, they were released because the government saw that the movement would not die. In 1988 the government recognized Solidarity and one year later, the Communist dominated government agreed to allow one third of the seats in the Polish congress to be open to non-Communist parties. Solidarity won nearly all of those seats. The military leader of Poland, General Jaruzelski, allowed the labor union leaders to form a government, the first led by non-Communists in 40 years. By 1990, Communism was dead in Poland, and Lech Walesa became the first popularly elected president since before World War II.

Poland has been one of the leading nations of the former East European bloc to become an integral part of western economics and politics. The country has been very successful, and it has thrown open its doors to visitors and the several million Poles who had immigrated over the decades prior to the war. There is a free exchange of ideas and commerce both, making Poland a very modern nation. The final capstone was when Poland joined the European Union and NATO. But like the United Kingdom, Denmark and Sweden, it has chosen not to use the Euro, remaining with its own national currency.

A BRIEF CITY HISTORY: The city of Gdańsk is a very historic and important Polish city. It dates to the 10th century. Its history during the medieval period is one of contest between local knights and the Polish crown, but in the mid 14th century, it became a part of the prosperous Hanseatic League. By the start of the 15th century, the city was under the control of the Polish king, however, the history of Poland has been one that has been closely tied to that of Prussia, and for long periods the country was ruled by the Germanic crown rather than its own. During the years of the renaissance, Gdańsk became a rich and important trading port, and this period is often seen as its golden age. There was much ethnic mixing as Germans, Poles, Jews and Dutch people mingled in its streets and markets. By 1772,

Gdańsk had declined, as Poland was partitioned between the German, Austro-Hungarian and Russian empires and Gdańsk became a part of Prussia, and ultimately part of the united German Empire in 1871. Other German ports such as Rostock and Hamburg overshadowed its importance.

Throughout so much of the city's later history, it was known as Danzig – the Germanic name that some people still use in reference to the port. It was only after World War I that Poland was allowed a narrow corridor to the Baltic and the city of Danzig was put under nominal authority of the League of Nations with Poland controlling its external affairs. And the Poles renamed it Gdańsk.

During the interim between the two world wars, Poland emerged as an independent nation, and Gdańsk uneasily became a major seaport along with Gdynia. It was here that German gunboats opened fire upon the port on September 1, 1939, thus igniting World War II. And as noted above, it was Poland that was totally overrun by both German and Russian forces over the next six years. The country paid a terrible price in blood and destruction of its infrastructure. Since Polish liberation from Germany, and with a readjustment of the borders, Gdańsk again became a major center for trade as well as for shipbuilding. It also then became a thorn in the side of the Communist authorities, as it was here that Solidarity began its agitation for a free Poland.

Because of its long association with the Hanseatic League, and its importance as a seaport, Gdańsk is a city richly endowed with great historic attractions. It has become one of the most popular tourist sites for those who cruise the Baltic Sea as well as among visitors who tour the major cities of Poland. Most of the important sites are located within the Old Town, which is much larger and more impressive than that of any other city in the eastern Baltic Sea region. And it is especially important when one considers that it was nearly all destroyed during World War II, yet lovingly and faithfully rebuilt after the war. Old photographs taken at the end of the war show the Old Town as simply a mass of rubble with a few crumbling walls. Yet it was restored faithfully and is a testament to great Polish pride.

I strongly urge everyone who will be visiting Gdańsk by cruise ship to sign up for one of the ship's walking tours of the Old Town. This is the best way to learn about the city through seeing its dedicated monumental buildings. Yes you can walk the Old Town on your own, but you will miss so much of the fascinating history that can only be related by one of the many guides.

THE PHYSICAL LAYOUT OF THE CITY OF GDAŃSK: Gdańsk and its neighboring port of Gdynia represent Poland's window on the Baltic. Today it is the fourth largest urban complex in Poland with a metropolitan population of just over 1,000,000 people. It is Poland's gateway to the world with regard to maritime pursuits, thus making it a major seaport city. Gdańsk Bay serves as the outlet for the Motlawa River, but the upper end of the river is connected ultimately to the Vistula so that barge traffic can carry goods from Warsaw to the coast. Thus it is the major port city for Warsaw, which is about 383 kilometers or 240 miles to the south of Gdańsk.

Gdańsk is quite a large city physically, as its suburbs do spread outward into the surrounding countryside. Between Gdańsk and Gdynia, a distance of 22 kilometers or 14 miles there is a string of suburban communities with the resort town of Sopot situated in the middle. These suburbs are not totally contiguous, and some are dominated over by large apartment blocks some of which date to the Communist Era mixed with small single-family homes.

The heart of Gdańsk lies along the Moltawa River with the historic Old Town right at its center. Although there is no actual wall around Old Town, its historic architecture dating back to the Hanseatic League is markedly different from the more modern structures beyond. And there are two dramatic old gates that do mark each end of the elegant Long Street that runs through the historic district. Despite its apparent antiquity, every bit of it was lovingly and carefully rebuilt after it was heavily bombed into rubble during World War II, not by its liberators but rather at the time it fell to Nazi forces in 1939. Remember it was here that the first battle of World War II was fought.

Few visitors ever leave the historic Old Town, as this is the main attraction of Gdańsk. The new city center is located just to the north of the historic center and it is a mix of Communist Era buildings with a handful of modern high-rises. Given the population of Gdańsk, it is not what one would expect because the suburban sprawl of the city has come with localized shopping districts and malls.

The main railroad lines all converge from north, south and east into a massive band of track that separates the Old Town and new city center from the spreading suburbs to the south and west. There is a very grand railway station built in the 19th century, but looking much older with its grand brick and stone facade.

The extensive port area lies to the northeast of the Old Town along the mouth of the Moltawa River. The Moltawa is actually a distributary of the Vistula River, which drains north from southern Poland, passing through the capital city of Warsaw. The geographic term distributary means that it is a branch of the lower end of a river that helps to drain the main river out to the sea or whatever larger body of water is the final destination. The harbor is very extensive and contains the shipyards that provide a great source of income for the city. And it was in the main shipyard that the Solidarity movement began the liberation of Poland from Communism.

The rival port for Gdańsk is the suburban city of Gdynia, located about 22 kilometers or 14 miles north along the coastline. The Polish government has spent a lot of money in building the infrastructure for the port, which is exceptionally modern and efficient. Prior to World War I, Gdynia was Poland's only window on the Baltic Sea while Gdańsk, still called Danzig, was a free trade port under the auspices of the League of Nations, yet claimed by Germany as theirs, and heavily populated with Germans. The narrow strip of land around Gdynia was often referred to as the Polish Corridor, and Germany was not pleased with the arrangement. Thus it was understandable that when the Nazi government decided upon an invasion, Gdańsk would be the first target, the opening salvo of the war on September 1, 1939 in the harbor of Gdańsk.

Like Gdańsk, Gdynia is also an old city, dating back to 1253 as an ancient fishing village. By the late 19th century, the city was a popular tourist spot with small guesthouses and cafes along its waterfront. The initial development of the seaport began in 1920, but the predominantly German residents of Gdańsk were hostile to the Polish authorities being so close to their territory. The Germans occupied the port of Gdynia in September 1939, as Nazi forces advanced across Poland. It became an important German naval base, and its shipyard served the Third Reich. There was once a concentration camp located just outside of Gdańsk, but it never developed an infamous reputation.

When the German withdrew in the face of the allied advance, they destroyed much of the port facilities in both Gdańsk and Gdynia. The Soviet Union saw to it that the borders of Poland were re adjusted to give the country an expanded window to the Baltic, thus making Gdynia and its larger neighbor Gdańsk a major economic and port center.

The modern city itself began to develop after the port was established, and by 1938, Gdynia was the most modern seaport on the Baltic Sea. Gdynia is still heavily industrialized and its architecture still reflects a strong measure of Communist Era development.

You will only see Gdynia if you are on board one of the large cruise ships, as this is where your ship will dock. But there is absolutely nothing in the city that is of interest to the average visitor. And most cruise lines will offer shuttle bus service to the Old Town area of Gdańsk for those guests who are not going on group tours that would be leaving from the docks in Gdynia.

Once in Gdańsk, there are numerous ways to get around and see all the sights. However, I must reiterate that the majority of what visitors come to see is in the relatively compact Old Town. The ways to see greater Gdańsk are:

* Ship sponsored tours, either by coach or on foot. Most of the Old Town can only be seen on foot. But many tours include the Solidarity Shipyards, the historic old religious site in Oliwa and the resort community of Sopot.

* If you wish to have the privacy and freedom of your own car and driver, the cruise line can arrange that for you, but at a relatively steep cost. To arrange for a private car and driver/guide on your own contact SIXT My Driver at *www.mydriver.com* for further information, rates and booking.

* Hop on hop off bus service exists in Gdańsk. If your cruise ship docks in Gdynia, you may need to take a ship shuttle bus into Gdańsk to board the hop on hop off bus. For ships docking in Gdańsk harbor you will still need to take a ship sponsored shuttle into the Old Town. The two routes (blue and red) begin and end their service at the Railway Station, which is a short distance to the northwest beyond the Old

Town. For further information contact *www.visitgdansk.com* for information, rates and booking.

* Many choose to simply take the ship shuttle from the dock into the Old Town and walk. It is a very enjoyable way to see Gdańsk. You can walk from the Old Town into the modern city center, which is immediately to the north, between the railway tracks and the river.

There is much to see in Gdańsk, most of the venues in the Old Town. Among the many sites that make greater Gdańsk popular are (shown in alphabetical order):

* European Center of Solidarity Movement - This modern museum is dedicated to the role of Gdańsk in modern labor movements and the role of Solidarity in the formation of the new Polish government. To reach this museum, you will need to take a taxi to **Plac Solidarności 1. The museum is open from 10 AM to 6 PM daily.**

* Gdańsk Town Hall - Located on Long Street in the Old Town, this building with its wood carved main staircase and other artistic touches reflects the glory days of the power of Gdańsk. The town hall is open from 10 AM to 4 PM, but on Tuesday it closes at 1 PM, Thursday at 6 PM and then is open Sunday 11 AM to 4 PM. The building is closed Monday.

* Gdańsk War Memorial - This absolutely moving memorial is built on a slight hill overlooking the entrance to the Gdańsk Harbor. Like all war memorials in Eastern Europe, this one is very poignant and evokes both a sadness and respect for the Polish people. If you are cruising on one of the small up market lines, your ship will dock adjacent to the memorial. If you are visiting off one of the mega ships, you will have to check and see if the memorial is part of any of the tours, otherwise it can only be reached by means of a private car, taxi or local tour. This memorial is generally included on any Westerplatte tour. If your ship docks in Gdańsk it will be tied op opposite the war memorial, however, because of the fences, it is a fair walk to get into the memorial on your own, but you can obtain excellent views from the ship's upper decks.

* Golden Gate - The arched entrance to the Old Town from the landward side, it is not as large as the Green Gate, but it is still a dynamic structure. It offers a dramatic entry into the Old Town and by itself, it is a magnificent piece of Hanseatic architecture capable of being viewed 24-hurs per day.

* Green Gate - This arched building stands as the gateway to the Old Town when coming from the riverside. It was once an aristocratic residence, but today it is the primary entry into the Old Town. You can tour the former residence Tuesday thru Saturday from 10 AM to 5 PM or simply enjoy its magnificent façade and walk through its passage onto the Long Street.

* Kosciol Mariacki – Saint Mary's Church, one of the city's old cathedrals reflecting the impact of the Roman Catholic faith upon Polish culture. It was built over the period of 1343 to 1542 and is the world's largest brick Gothic church. The cathedral

in Uppsala, Sweden is second in size. The church dominates the skyline of the Old Town and you will have no difficulty in finding it if you choose to visit on your own. The church is open to visitors from 9 AM to 8:30 PM daily.

* Long Street and Long Market – This is the most beautiful sight in Gdańsk, starting at the Golden Gate and ending at the Green Gate. This was once home to the richest residences in Gdańsk, many of the buildings dating back to medieval times. The architecture is one in which there are narrow facades and steep gables and parapets atop each building. The Long Street is the main feature of any guided walking tour of Old Town.

* National Maritime Museum - The museum consists of three distinct parts, the main museum, the granary and the crane. It details the importance of Gdańsk as a major port in the 18th and 19th centuries. The museum can be reached on foot from the Old Town by walking along the Moltawa River to **Tokarska 21/25. The museum is open from 10 AM to 7 PM daily thru August, then from 10 AM to 4 PM Tuesday thru Friday and from 10 AM to 6 PM on weekends thru November.**

* Neptune Fountain – Located in the heart of the city, this fountain was cast in 1615 and symbolizes the city's bond with the sea. The fountain stands in front of the Town Hall and is a main feature of the Long Street.

* Oliwa Cathedral – A magnificent cathedral dating to the 13th century, originally built in Gothic style, but later rebuilt with baroque design after being destroyed by a major fire. This is one of the most magnificent of cathedrals in Poland. It is located about 6 miles from the city center in the small suburban town of Oliwa, and is often visited by tours offered by the major cruise lines. If you are not on a tour, you may reach the cathedral by taxi, as Oliwa is a well-recognized destination. The cathedral is open from 9 AM to 5 PM weekdays, 9 AM to 3:30 PM Saturday and 2 to 5:30 PM Sunday. No visitors are permitted during mass.

* Sopot - The town of Sopot located between Gdańsk and Gdynia is a very important part of the combined urban region. This is the Baltic Sea playground for all of Poland, having many hotels, spas and broad sandy beaches. Some cruise lines offer a half-day tour to Sopot, but I do not recommend it because you miss so much of the history and architectural beauty of the city itself. Only visit Sopot if you want to enjoy a beach resort and if you have been to Gdańsk before.

* Ulitza Mariacki – Saint Mary's Street is one of the most beautiful streets in the city, lined with many old houses that possess a rich architectural heritage, some dating to the Hanseatic League, and all beautifully restored after the end of World War II. Again this street will also be featured in any guided walking tour.

* Westerplatte – This is the most important site in Gdańsk when it comes to contemporary history. It was on this narrow peninsula in Gdańsk Bay that German naval guns fired upon the city on the morning of September 1, 1939, supposedly in response to what the Nazi government claimed were Polish border incursions into Germany. As a result of this action, World War II officially began. There is really

not a lot to see here, but it is very poignant to stand on the spot where the opening salvo of World War II was fired. You can only reach Westerplatte either on a tour, private excursion with your own car and driver/guide or taxi. There are several small private tour operators in It is too far from where the ship's shuttle bus will drop off guests. The small museum is open from 10 AM thru 4 PM daily until October. The outdoor exhibit on the spot where World War II began is open during daylight hours as is the great World War II memorial.

CUISINE OF GDAŃSK: Despite its long association with Germany and the large number of German people who lived in Gdańsk, its cultural heritage is now very much Polish. And as a part of that heritage, food plays a major role. Polish cooking is rich in its diversity, elegant in its presentation and also includes some of the best-baked goods you will find anywhere in Europe. Many types of soup are popular in Poland. Borsch is similar to that of Russia, yet it has a definite Polish twist. And Zhurkek is considered a national soup, made with milk, fermented rye, carrots and spicy sausage. Rolled cabbage stuffed with pork or chicken and rice is cooked in a savory broth that has a both sweet and sour taste. There are also small stuffed pastry dumplings known as pirogue, which can be filled with meat, potato or cheese and covered with onions sautéed in butter or with fresh sour cream. Rich and savory sausages are served with cabbage and noodles as another popular dish. And to top off the meal, there are delicate strudels stuffed with apple, cherry or poppy seed and raisin that just melt in the mouth. All are a part of Polish cuisine, which though similar to Russian, has a greater degree of finesse. Every visitor should sample the cuisine and is sure to enjoy the flavors of Poland.

Gdańsk is filled with restaurants because of the number of visitors who come to the Old Town. There are dozens of restaurants lining the Long Street and also along the waterfront. As usual, I have my favorites, and they are based upon my combined Polish and Russian heritage. The best restaurants in Gdańsk that are truly Polish are to be found outside of the Old Town in various residential districts of the city. But these are impossible to get to without either knowledge of the language or the services of a car and driver/guide. The restaurants inside the Old Town definitely cater to tourists and the majority does not expect return guests. Of the restaurants in Old Town that I have tried, there are only a handful I feel comfortable recommending:

* Barylka - Located along the Moltawa Embankment and open for lunch and dinner, Barylka pays careful attention to presenting traditional Polish cuisine in an atmosphere that is both sophisticated, yet has the feel of a country inn. Their menu is complete and offers all of the traditional dishes I noted above. They do not have an extensive dessert menu, but by the time you are finished with the meal, you will not have much room. They are open for lunch and dinner daily, serving daily from 10 AM to 11 PM.

* Pieroarnia Mandu Centrum – Locat Ulitsa Elzbietanska # 4-8, in the heart of Old Town, this is a must if you have never tried Pierogi, those small dumplings that are to Polish cuisine what fish and chips are to British cuisine. There are so many types of pierogi and they can be boiled, baked or fried. This restaurant is a magnet for

those who love the national dish. The food and service are incredible. If you have no preference, I recommend cheese pierogi smothered in sour cream – high in cholesterol, but you are on vacation. They are open daily from 11 AM to 10 PM.

* Pomelo Bistro – In the heart of Old Town at Ulitsa Ogarna 121-122, this is a very popular and genuine Polish restaurant. Their diverse menu covers quite an array of Polish dishes, all expertly prepared and served in an impeccable manner. Like all Polish dishes, the food is quite hearty and not light if you are watching your diet, but oh so good to the taste. It would be a shame to visit Gdańsk and not try the mouth-watering cuisine. And this is a good choice. They are open Monday thru Thursday from 8 AM to 9 PM starting with traditional breakfast. Friday and Saturday they open at 9 PM and remain open until 10 PM. Sunday they open at 9 AM and close at 9 PM.

* Restauracja Bazar – Located across the Motlawa River from the Green Gate, at Ulitsa Szafarnia # 6, which is facing the island in the middle of the channel at the north end. Their diverse menu will provide you with a great selection of Polish dishes from which to choose. The cuisine is genuine, well prepared and nicely served. They are open daily from Noon to 10 PM.

SHOPPING: Within Old Town there are dozens of shops and stalls selling a mix of tourist kitsch and local handcrafts. Polish lace, embroidery and dolls are traditional items that can range in price from a few dollars into hundreds depending upon size and quality. There are also artists who will be selling small to medium size watercolors, but you must be careful to make certain that you are not buying a print, but an original instead. The most commonly purchased item by visitors is amber jewelry. Once again the old motto of buyer beware applies, as fake amber looks as good as real amber to the untrained eye. It is best to purchase amber in a reputable looking shop and charge your purchase so as to have grounds for entering the amount into a dispute if you later determine that you have been sold something that is not as represented. I personally have no interest in amber. It is nice to look at, but it does not entice me, and thus I have no real opinion as to whether it is a worthwhile purchase. I do know it is relatively rare and that the Baltic Sea region is where most quality amber is to be found.

There are two shopping centers in Gdańsk, but both are outside of Old Town, necessitating a taxi ride or if you have a car and driver/guide you then can reach either or both. One is a traditional marketplace and the second is the largest modern mall in central Gdańsk:

* Galeria Handlowa Madison - This is the largest of the modern shopping malls in Gdańsk, and it is located in the heart of the new central business district at Rajska 10, due north from Hala Targowa about half a mile. This mall contains four floors of shops and cafes, open from 9 AM to 9 PM every day except Sunday when it closes at 2 PM. The shops carry a variety of European and Polish brands at a range of prices to please every budget.

* Hala Targowa - This is the old public market of Gdańsk. It sells a mix of fresh

produce, meats, breads and baked goods along with clothing and has a few shops that do sell local handcrafts. But it is a fun place to visit because you will be mingling with locals and seeing how they shop. Surprisingly many guide books do recommend Hala Targowa as a place to at least be seen. It is walking distance from the Long Street in Old Town. Just walk north from Old Town to Plac Dominkański. It is open from 9 AM to 6 PM weekdays, 9 AM to 3 PM Saturday and closed Sunday.

FINAL NOTES: For most people who do not have any Polish heritage, Gdańsk will be your first impression. And it should be a positive one. The city's Old Town has been lovingly rebuilt to the look of medieval and Hanseatic times, a level of authenticity hard to match. Yes it is somewhat commercialized, but there is a definite attempt to present folk dancing, local crafts and good Polish food with an air of graciousness. If you want to experience a more realistic aspect of life in Gdańsk, then you need to walk beyond the Golden Gate out into the modern downtown of the city. Here you will be outside the normal tourist area and therefore mingling with Polish people as they go about their everyday lives. You will find that Poland is a modern country, but one where traditional values have not been lost.

A visit to Warsaw, Poland's vibrant capital and largest city is not possible during the normal eight to 10-hour visit of most cruise ships. But many guests on board ship who have a Polish heritage, and those seeking to explore one of the major countries of Eastern Europe will often add onto their holiday by taking a trip to Warsaw or Kraków after their cruise ends. For this reason, I have included a chapter on Warsaw since it is becoming one of the most visited cities of the former Eastern Bloc.

GDAŃSK MAPS

THE CITY OF GDAŃSK

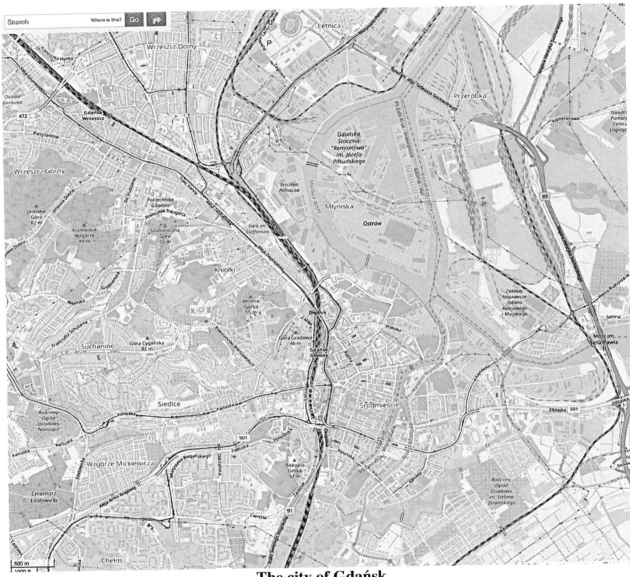

The city of Gdańsk

This map is best viewed directly from OpenStreetMap.com on your personal device where it can be expanded or one specific area can be enlarged. Given the format of this book, it is impossible to display maps with the level of detail you might wish to have while actually out exploring the city. But the OpenStreetMap maps used directly are the tool I always rely upon.

OLD GDAŃSK

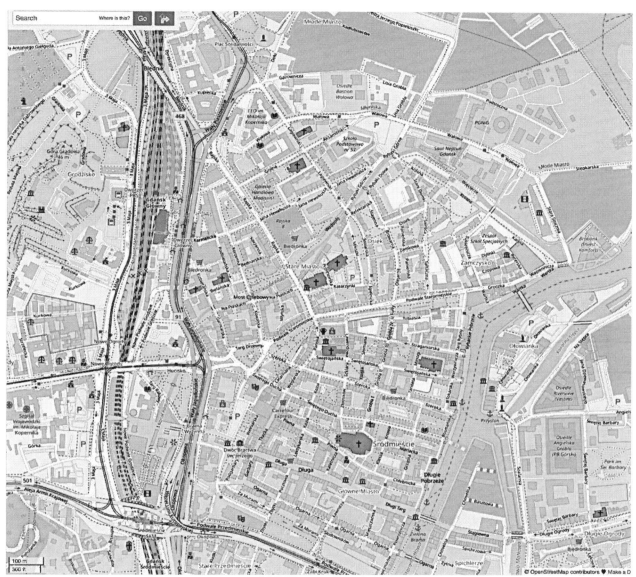

Old Town Gdańsk

This map is best viewed directly from OpenStreetMap.com on your personal device where it can be expanded or one specific area can be enlarged. Given the format of this book, it is impossible to display maps with the level of detail you might wish to have while actually out exploring the city. But the OpenStreetMap maps used directly are the tool I always rely upon.

THE CITY OF GDYNIA

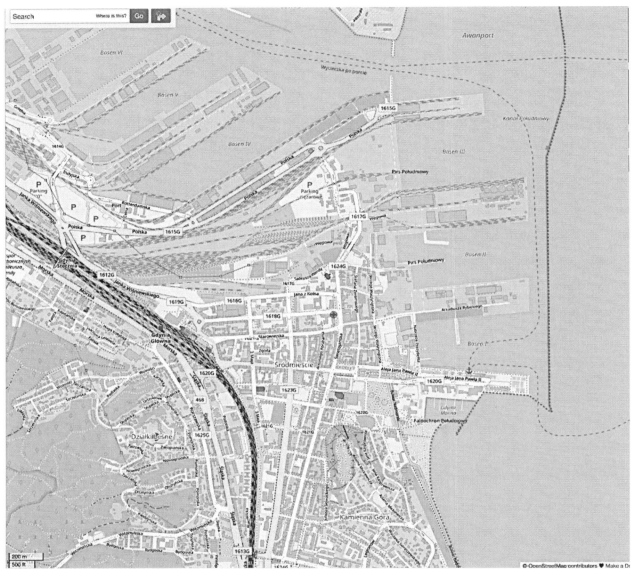

The city of Gdynia

This map is best viewed directly from OpenStreetMap.com on your personal device where it can be expanded or one specific area can be enlarged. Given the format of this book, it is impossible to display maps with the level of detail you might wish to have while actually out exploring the city. But the OpenStreetMap maps used directly are the tool I always rely upon.

THE RESORT CITY OF SOPOT

The resort city of Sopot

This map is best viewed directly from OpenStreetMap.com on your personal device where it can be expanded or one specific area can be enlarged. Given the format of this book, it is impossible to display maps with the level of detail you might wish to have while actually out exploring the city. But the OpenStreetMap maps used directly are the tool I always rely upon.

154

Gdańsk seen from the air flying in from Warsaw

The Golden Gate leading onto the Long Street of Old Town Gdańsk

The Golden Gate connects with the new city center

The Green Gate facing the river at the east edge of Old Town Gdańsk

The Green Gate from the Long Street side

The Long Street between the two gates

One of the many elegant examples of Hanseatic League architecture

The massive destruction of Old Town at the end of World War II

The magnificent Town Hall on the Long Street

Neptune's Fountain outside of the Old Town Hall

Saint Mary's Cathedral dominates over Old Town Gdańsk

The Moltawa River flows along the edge of Old Town Gdańsk

A quiet back street in the Old Town

An elegant Old Town doorway

In the modern city center of Gdańsk

19ᵗʰ century buildings in the modern city center

The monument to the Solidarity Labor uprising< (Work of Georg Denda, CC BY SA 3.0, Wikimedia.org)

Monument to the fallen in World War II, (Work of Kuuba 123, CC BY SA 4.0, Wikimedia.org)

The massive Gdańsk harbor and shipyard facilities

WARNEMUNDE & BERLIN, GERMANY

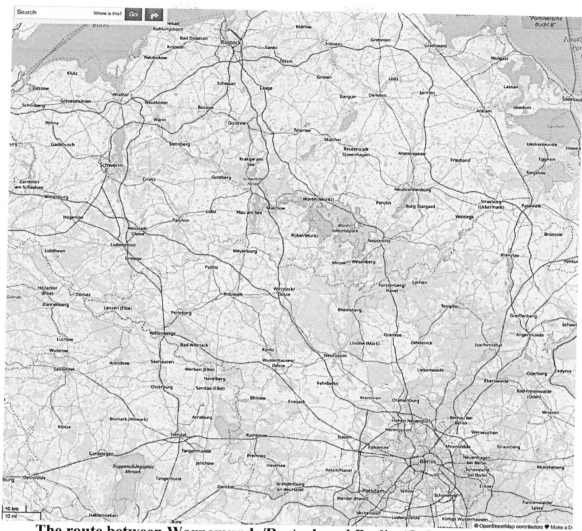

The route between Warnemunde/Rostock and Berlin (© OpenStreetMap contributors)

Warnemunde and its larger neighbor Rostock are the major German seaports that serve the inland capital city of Berlin, one of Europe's truly great cities. Berlin is located 209 kilometers or 130 miles to the south of Warnemunde via the Autobahn, Germany's superb and not to be rivaled system of divided express highways. The Autobahn is the original freeway first built by the Nazi regime back in the 1930's. One needs to be prepared for a fast ride if traffic is light, as in Germany there are few speed limits and drivers travel along principal roads at high speed. Depending upon traffic of the day, a trip into the heart of Berlin should only take an average 90 to 120 minutes.

THE NATURAL SETTING OF GERMANY: Germany, known as Deutschland, contains 357,022 square kilometers or 137,847 square miles and has a population of over 80,700,000. The reunited country's landmass is about the size of the American state of Montana, slightly larger than Poland. But it is a more densely populated nation containing many major cities. It is the most populous nation in Europe apart from Russia, which of course spans both Europe and Asia. Germany is essentially the powerhouse of Europe, its most prosperous and highly industrialized nation.

Part of the German success lies in its land. Southern Germany borders the Alps. This is a beautiful region, known as Bavaria, rich in minerals, timber and a favored tourist destination. From the Alps, the Rhine River flows through the western part of Germany. With its tributaries, the greater Rhine Valley is a fertile region that offers many agricultural riches. Central Germany possesses a mix of forest and farmland in country that is gently rolling. Along the eastern border with the Czech Republic is the famous Black Forest, one of Europe's natural gems. Northern German is part of the North European Plain, that glacial till that gives most of Poland its great fertility. The climates vary from mild and wet in the northwest to cold and snowy in winter along the Polish border to moderately cold and wet in the south, with snow at higher elevations. The key word is wet, meaning that Germany is a luxuriant country. This means that it is highly productive, especially when one adds the German technology and drive to make itself productive. Approximately 30 percent of the country is under cultivation, but given the large population, imports of many foodstuffs are still important. Germany is one of the world's industrialized nations, and like Japan, it must import many of its raw materials. But German technology and precision quality have combined to make her products in demand worldwide.

Germany is also blessed with large reserves of coal, which fueled the industrial revolution of the 19th century. Today's German industries rely more upon oil, hydro power and wind energy, so its coal deposits are of less value. Apart from coal, the country is not overly rich in minerals, but it has made up for its lack of raw materials by possessing a highly skilled and innovative population. Both Germany and Japan have used their brain power to compensate for the lack of natural resources, and as a result they are the powerhouses of their respective continents.

Berlin is located in the North European Plain, situated along the River Spree, which bisects the city. A mix of woodland, glacial lakes and well-developed agricultural land surrounds Berlin, and the entire region is essentially flat to just gently rolling. Being located in the northern part of the country and some distance from the Atlantic Ocean, Berlin still does receive a significant amount of winter snow. Summers are generally mild, but there can be periods of very warm and humid weather.

A BRIEF GERMAN HISTORY: Visiting Berlin without an understanding of the history of Germany and the role the city has played will take away much of the meaning of what you will see. The city's overall flavor, its many fine buildings and the distinct architectural differences between what was from 1945 until 1990 East Berlin can better be appreciated with a basic knowledge of modern history and how it is rooted in Germany's past.

Most visitors often see Germans as somewhat aloof, even arrogant. But if this perception has any merit, it is in part because they are a highly creative nation. German education is rigid and places emphasis not only upon the sciences, but also upon literature, art and music as well as psychology and philosophy. Think of the great scholars, composers, musicians, doctors and scientists that have come from Germany. The list is most impressive.

Visitors often think of the Germans as one people with a long history as nation. This is not true on either account. Germans are somewhat unified in purpose and they have possessed a strong nationalism since the late 19th century, but there are intense regional differences in daily customs and even in dialect. And since World War II, Germany has seen the influx of many workers from Italy, Turkey and Greece. Today in 2018, there has been a massive influx of refugees and those looking to better their lives, people coming from Africa and the Middle East. The tide of this influx is massive and is causing problems for many of the nations southeast of Germany where the refuges land by boat and then attempt to make the journey northward with Germany as their goal.

The nation retains very strong regulations regarding citizenship, primarily aimed at not diluting the cultural identity of Germany. Yet based upon humanitarian grounds the government indicated in the refugee crisis of 2015-16 it was willing to absorb up to 1,000,000 refugees and asylum seekers. This has not been meeting with the full support of the populace, as many Germans fear diluting their culture. It was this ethnic nationalism, fueled by Adolph Hitler's concept of "Deutschland uber alls," translated to mean Germany over everyone, that got the country into so much trouble. There is a pride in being German that is justified, but today it is tempered with reason. It is hard to overlook the great spirit of the people and their ability to have risen from the ashes of World War II to become Europe's most powerful economic force.

The Germanic tribes were rather warlike during the days of the Roman Empire, but around the start of our calendar, the Romans conquered much of southern Germany. Following the fall of Rome, the Franks, the southern Germans, formed an empire that extended well into France and as far north as the Netherlands. The famous Charlemagne becomes Holy Roman Emperor in 800, uniting most of the Franks under his domain. By 843, the Frankish lands were divided into three kingdoms, the eastern kingdom becoming Germany in 919. But Germany was essentially nothing more than a loose confederation of semi-independent principalities, however, calling itself an empire.

By 1438, Austria emerges as the dominant Germanic kingdom, and by 1648 the Netherlands and Switzerland secede. Prussia emerges by 1756 as the second great power after Austria, but eventually becomes the dominant Germanic force militarily, and during the mid 1700's, under Frederick the Great it grew to be a major power, having great influence over the lesser Germanic principalities. As a result of the Napoleonic War, the German Empire degenerated into a loose confederacy with no one kingdom being the dominant member, Prussia and Austria remained somewhat apart.

When Napoleon was defeated, the Vienna Congress in 1815 unified all of the German states, but this did not last long, as Austria and Prussia fought in 1867, resulting in Bavaria and Austria remaining outside of the newly formed state. In the 1870-71 Franco Prussian War, Prussia successfully united the various principalities into a united German Empire. From this point on, Germany took an aggressive stand in terms of expanding and building its world influence. Colonies were established in Africa, the South Pacific and Germany began to take an active role as one of the trade powers dominating China. Although a monarchy, Germany developed a parliament and Otto von Bismarck became the powerful chancellor. While Bismarck was establishing a German power base, winning respect and improving trade, the Kaiser (German word for Caesar) worked toward building up the German military. By 1914, Germany seized upon the assassination of the Austro-Hungarian archduke, siding with Austria in a war against Serbia. This drew in Italy on the German-Austrian side and Britain and France on the Russian side. World War I began. Later the United States joined the allies to help defeat Germany.

Germany was left in chaos after the war. The Treaty of Versailles stripped Germany of its colonies, forced it to pay reparations and it was not allowed to station any military troops west of the Rhine River. The country went into depression, the Deutschmark plummeted in value and the government became very unstable. The Kaiser was forced to abdicate, leaving the country in a state of near anarchy. The country also lost territory to France and Poland, taking away valuable industries and agricultural lands.

As social unrest and economic failure plagued the country, Adolph Hitler and his Nazi Party began to take advantage of the situation. At first Hitler was put down by the government and even spent time in prison, but ultimately he used the powers of both persuasion and brutality to rise to dominance. In 1933, the Nazi Party won the election and Adolph Hitler was sworn in as Chancellor by the aging president Paul von Hindenburg. Once in power, Hitler and his advisors set about to turn Germany into a dictatorship based upon the concepts of racism and nationalism. To foster these strong ideals, rooted in Nordic mythology, the Jews became the major target of German ire, blamed for all the post war ills. Other ethnic groups such as Poles and Gypsies were also singled out for persecution, as were the infirm and mentally handicapped.

Hitler sent German troops across the Rhine in 1935, reclaiming the Saar region that had been given to France. The French and British did nothing to stop him. Reports of oppression and persecution were not totally believed outside of Germany, and Hitler had a free hand to carry out his actions. During the 1936 summer Olympic games held in Berlin, Hitler snubbed African-American superstar Jessie Owens by refusing to present him with his gold medal, giving everyone outside of Germany some insight into his attitudes toward the outside world. But the United States did not even protest.

In 1938, German troops marched into Austria, claiming that it was truly German. Many Austrians welcomed the union with Germany, but most feared the consequences. The following year, Hitler demanded the western part of Czechoslovakia, the region in which many Germans lived. The British Prime Minister Neville Chamberlain conceded based upon a promise of friendship. Then on September 1, 1939, Germany used the pretext of the Polish forces having fired upon a German border outpost and invaded Poland and World War II began because Britain and France had pledged to defend the Polish people.

Suffice it to say that Germany reaped a whirlwind of destruction, as the Allies advanced from both east and west. The country was left utterly devastated. Berlin was nothing more than a bombed out ruin with few buildings remaining unscathed. The fighting in the streets of Berlin in the last few weeks of the war was of terrible ferocity, and it was the Red Army that ultimately claimed the victory of capturing the city. And this partly strengthened their claim to much of the territory of what would become East Germany. The Berlin you visit today is a totally rebuilt city, but many buildings were lovingly restored to their old nature, thus making it hard to believe that in 1945 they lay in ruin. Even the Reichstag has been totally rebuilt and once again serves as the German Parliament. This did not occur until after the 1990 reunification, and symbolizes the new Germany.

The post war recovery in West Germany under American, British and French protection was rapid. East Germany became a Soviet dominated state with typical Communist oppression. The victors divided the city of Berlin, but the western half of the city was unified under its own government. But being behind the Iron Curtain, Russia forced a blockade of rail and highways in 1948, which the Allies broke by a massive airlift.

By 1949, the west was unified into the Federal Republic of Germany while the east became the German Democratic Republic. The Soviet Union had troops stationed in the east, and in 1961 they began construction on a wall to ring West Berlin and keep the people of the GDR prisoners in their own country by not allowing them an escape route via West Berlin. The wall became a notorious landmark of oppression. When John F. Kennedy visited Berlin, he stood near the wall and declared that, "Ich bin ein Berliner," saying he was a Berliner. America would not abandon the people of this surrounded city.

The year 1990 brought about the collapse of the GDR, and the wall began to come down. At last Germany could be reunited as one country. But the cost to the West in Deutschmark was tremendous, as the prosperous West had to share its wealth in the rehabilitation of the east.

The 1990 reunification with former Communist East Germany was costly to the economy of West Germany and did foster some resentment. As a reunified nation, the country has been able to expand its industrial and agricultural output greatly, and it is now the most important economic power on the continent. Germany's economy sets the stage for the European Union, and in today's time of economic troubles with countries such as Greece on the verge of bankruptcy, it has been the German government that has played the most major role in holding the European Union together. The role of Germany as the leader of the European economy combined with its government's generosity in allowing almost 1,000,000 displaced refugees from the Middle East and Africa to settle has caused quite a bit of dissention within the general populace. The current government of Angela Merkel has come under severe criticism for its actions. There is quite a backlash today from those who want the government to consider Germans first and refugees second, similar to the attitudes being seen in the United States.

\

THE PHYSICAL LAYOUT OF WARNEMUNDE AND ROSTOCK: The beachfront town of Warneumnde and the industrial city of Rostock, which is about 20 kilometers or 12 miles farther up the wide, broad Unterwarnow River forming the harbor combine to create one significant urban landscape with around 250,000 residents. Warnemunde is a small town that is primarily a Baltic Sea beach resort, though its history dates back to 1200 when it was founded as a small fishing village. Today with a resident population of just over 8,000, it plays host to thousands of visitors, mainly German, who come for summer holidays. Being that it is at the point where the harbor begins combined with its many restaurant and commercial amenities, it was the perfect location to build a cruise ship terminal. It is here that ships dock generally for a long day starting at around 7 AM and lasting until 10 or 11 PM. This gives the cruise lines sufficient time to operate a variety of tours to Berlin, which is the main focus of the port call. Some cruise lines charter a private train for the trip into Berlin, as the railway station in Warnemunde is directly opposite the cruise terminal. But other cruise lines have chartered busses, since via the Autobahn the travel time is quicker than by train.

Rostock is connected to Warnemunde by a local commuter rail train that leaves about every 20 minutes, the journey taking about the same amount of time. Rostock is a major industrial and port city with over 200,000 residents. Much of the residential portion of the city was built in the post-World War II period under Communism and is still rather uniform and drab. But the inner city of Rostock, which saw extensive rebuilding after the war, is faithful to its earlier centuries of history dating all the way to the Hanseatic League.

The port cities of Warnemunde and Rostock were once within the German Democratic Republic. A visitor there three decades ago would have found them rather drab with massive, gray apartment blocks. Shops were few, and goods were scares. The government was repressive and personal liberties limited. These would not have been interesting cities to visit. Rostock was once the only major port city for the German Democratic Republic, sharing the same harbor as Warnemunde. Rostock became a major manufacturing center while Warnemunde saw a significant amount of shipbuilding. During the Nazi build up leading to World War II, Rostock was an important ship building center and was also home to the Heinkel Nord airplane manufacturing plant where one of the earliest prototype jet aircraft was developed.

Today these two cities are still major ports, and shipbuilding and other industrial activities are still important. But there is a new spirit that has taken over. Warneumnde has returned to its original role as a summer seaside resort with many hotels, guesthouses and restaurants. It bustles with thousands of visitors, especially on the weekend, as it is an easy journey by car from Berlin or Hamburg. And on days when cruise ships dock, additional thousands of visitors crowd its small streets with people eager to spend their money. Rostock is still a major manufacturing center, but it is also an important academic center as well as being the major retail hub for northeastern Germany. During the German Democratic Republic era, Rostock was the major port for East Berlin and a center for diversified manufacturing. It was during this era that many of the old Hanseatic and later old buildings were faithfully restored because during World War II Rostock suffered severe damage from aerial bombing

WHAT TO SEE AND IN WARNEMUNDE: Today Warnemunde is a thriving beachfront city with an inner town center that is typical architecturally of a small German seaside community. There are many fine restaurants, bakeries and gift shops catering to those who come to enjoy its beach and small pleasure boat harbor. But apart from taking a walk around, browsing the shops or having a meal, there is essentially nothing for ship passengers to do in Warnemunde that warrants the long period of the port call.

The commuter rail line connecting Warnemunde with the larger and industrial city of Rostock does give those not visiting Berlin or any other venue outside of the port a chance to at least see a bit more of the metropolitan area. Most of the cruise lines do offer a four-hour bus tour into Rostock, often returning by small tour boat. But for those who wish to sightsee on their own, it is very easy to take the train into Rostock and then explore the older quarter of this comfortable city.

A few of the more up market cruise lines do offer bus tours to the beautiful and historic Schwerin Castle, a two-hour journey to the west. Schwerin is the ancient capital of Mecklenburg, one of the northern states of Germany. And its castle plus the beautiful lake around which the city of Schwerin is built makes for a way to spend five to six hours on tour.

The vast majority of ship passengers generally opt for one of the various one-day tours to Berlin. Some cruise lines charter a train for the journey while others use motor coaches. The vast majority of trips to Berlin are long, leaving just after docking and returning to the ship around 10 PM. But guests find the trip rewarding and do not complain about the long day's activity.

For those who will not travel to Berlin, I am providing information of taking a short trip either by group motor coach, riverboat or train into Rostock. These journeys can be made under the auspices of the cruise line, as a group tour, or very easily on your own. Once in Rostock, if on your own, it is easy to simply walk and enjoy the sights. There are no hop on hop off busses in Warnemunde or Rostock.

* If on your own, you can take the commuter train from the Warnemunde train station opposite the docks into Rostock and return. Tickets are purchased on the platform from an automated machine and trains run continuously. It is also possible to travel by comfortable passenger ferry one way or both, enjoying the sights of the

busy harbor. Boats run on a frequent schedule. For more information on using the harbor ferry check on line at *www.blaue-flotte.de* and then you can plan either a combined rail-ferry transfer or use one or the other for the round trip.

* Private cars with a driver/guide can be arranged through your cruise line, or privately by visiting online to Sixtmydriver at *www.mydriver.com* for rates and booking information. You can also inquire as to the cost of doing a private limousine tour to Berlin. But I can tell you now, it will be very expensive.

WHAT TO SEE AND DO IN ROSTOCK: Rostock dates back to the days of the Hanseatic League and its city center contains several streets with buildings that date back to the as early as the 14th century when it was the largest city in what is now northern Germany. This Old Town district merges with the new and modern buildings of the Rostock city center. There are two major medieval churches, and part of the town wall and one main tower still remain.

For those who chose to visit Rostock on their own it is a simple matter of walking from the cruise terminal to the railway station and taking the commuter train, which runs about every twenty minutes. Then from the Rostock Banhoff (train station) a local tram takes you into the city center at no extra charge. But apart from walking around the Old Town center, there are only a few nahir venues to visit in Rostock. These include (in alphabetical order):

* **Das Kulturhistorische Museum** – In the city center as Klosterhof # 7, this former historic old convent now houses the city's history museum. It is definitely worthy of a visit because it does provide you with a background as to the history and growth of Rostock. The museum is open Tuesday thru Sunday from 10 AM to 6 PM.

* **Neuer Markt** – This is the central market square in the heart of Rostock. It is surrounded by a collection of very beautiful buildings from the Hanseatic period of the city's history when it was a major trade center and includes the Town Hall and numerous shops and cafes. It is where the tram will stop when you come from the railway station upon arrival.

* **Sankt Mariem Kirche** – This is the 13th century brick cathedral that has been beautifully restored. It also has a fascinating astronomical clock on display. It has been quite faithfully restored and represents the role of the Catholic faith in this part of Germany. The church is located at Am Ziegenmarkt # 4 just north of the market square where most people alight from the tram to visit the city center. No specific hours are posted, but it is open during daylight hours unless a special service is being held.

WHAT TO SEE AND DO IN WARNEMUNDE: Warnemunde is technically a part of the greater city of Rostock, yet because it is located on the other side of the large harbor, it maintains its separate identity. This small beach resort has been popular among German visitors for the past two centuries, and it is where the cruise ships dock just inside the entrance to the main harbor. During the Communist Era, the residents of East Germany had no other resort on the Baltic other than

Warneumnde. There are few actual sights of significance, but it is a delightful place in which to walk around if you plan to stay close to the cruise ship.

* The only significant landmark worthy of note is the dominant lighthouse that sits at the entrance to the harbor. This lighthouse is 36 meters or 118 feet high and offers spectacular views over the surrounding coast and town. It was built in 1896 and dominates the skyline. The lighthouse is open to those who want to climb to the top between 10 AM and 7 PM daily.

DINING IN ROSTOCK OR WARNEMUNDE: Rostock is not specifically oriented toward catering to large numbers of foreign visitors. Therefore, its restaurants are quite genuine, but you may have a bit of a language problem. If you are willing to overcome this possibility, it is a nice place for lunch when you visit on your own. I recommend the following:

* Rathskeller12 – Located in the Neuer Markt, or market square at # 1. It is a superb traditional German restaurant serving a variety of dishes prepared along time honored lines. You can choose from seafood, meat and poultry dishes. The service is very good. They are open weekdays from 11:30 AM to Midnight, Saturday from 10 AM to Midnight and Sunday from 9:30 AM to 5 PM.

There are so many cafes lining the boardwalk in Warnemunde that the selection is infinite. The main specialty is fresh seafood, but other German dishes are offered. Most, however, have their menus written in German and many waiters do not speak English, but will be as helpful as possible. And the food is great. My favorite is:

* Restaurant Carls located Muenlenstrasse # 28 in the central shopping district. This is a traditional German restaurant, but it also offers healthy vegetarian dishes. They offer fresh seafood, Weinerschnitzel and an assortment of other popular entrees. The restaurant is open daily from11:30 AM to 10 PM.

ROSTOCK-WARNEMUNDE MAPS

THE ROSTOCK REGION

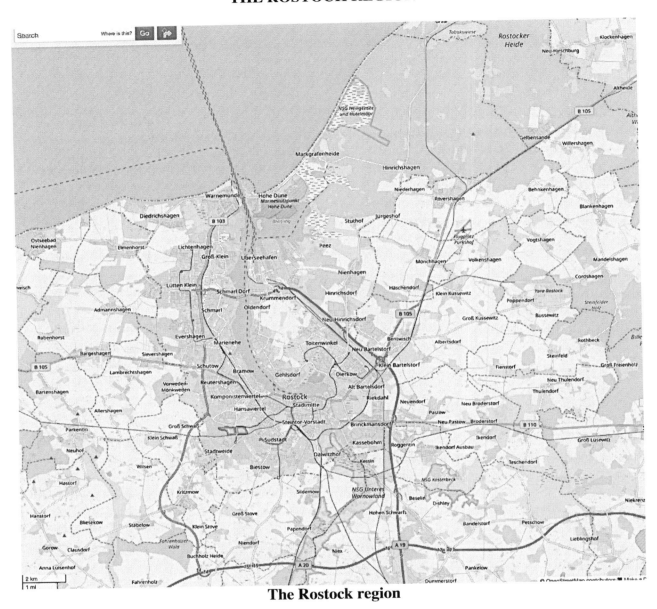

The Rostock region

This map is best viewed directly from OpenStreetMap.com on your personal device where it can be expanded or one specific area can be enlarged. Given the format of this book, it is impossible to display maps with the level of detail you might wish to have while actually out exploring the city. But the OpenStreetMap maps used directly are the tool I always rely upon.

THE PORT OF WARNEMUNDE

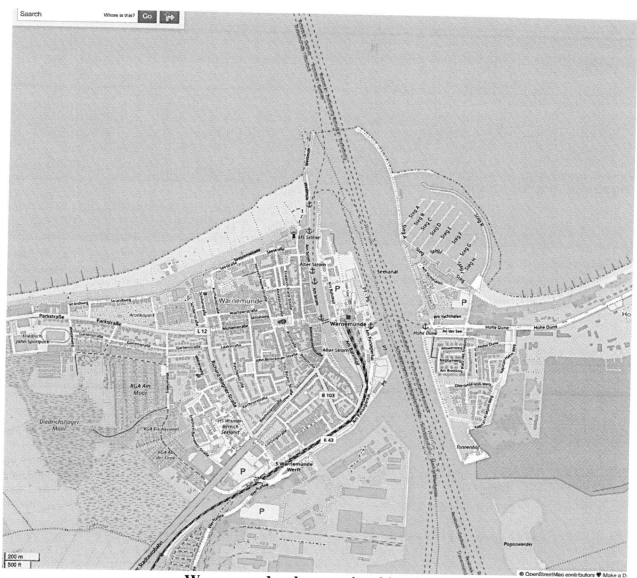

Warnemunde where cruise ships dock

This map is best viewed directly from OpenStreetMap.com on your personal device where it can be expanded or one specific area can be enlarged. Given the format of this book, it is impossible to display maps with the level of detail you might wish to have while actually out exploring the city. But the OpenStreetMap maps used directly are the tool I always rely upon.

THE CITY OF ROSTOCK

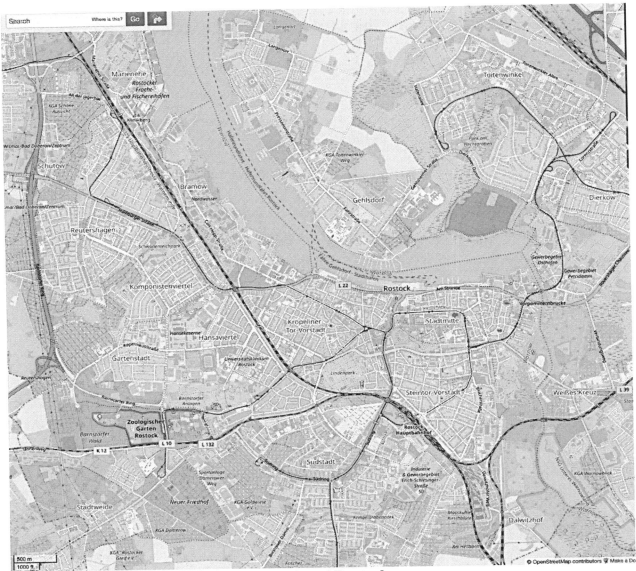

The city of Rostock

This map is best viewed directly from OpenStreetMap.com on your personal device where it can be expanded or one specific area can be enlarged. Given the format of this book, it is impossible to display maps with the level of detail you might wish to have while actually out exploring the city. But the OpenStreetMap maps used directly are the tool I always rely upon.

THE HEART OF ROSTOCK

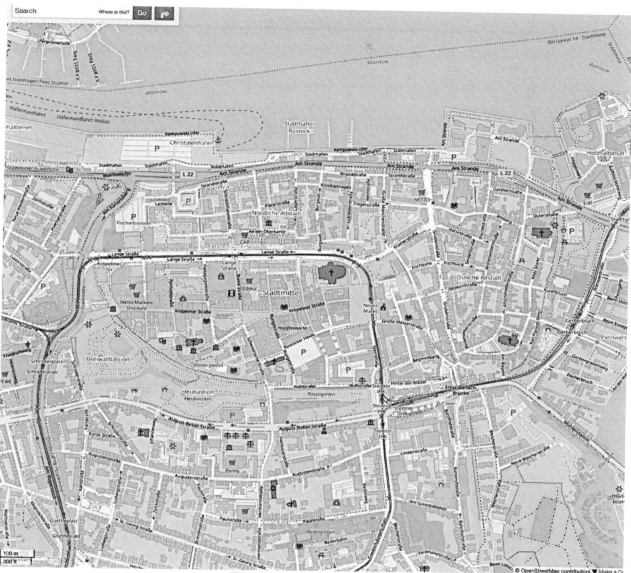

The Rostock city center

This map is best viewed directly from OpenStreetMap.com on your personal device where it can be expanded or one specific area can be enlarged. Given the format of this book, it is impossible to display maps with the level of detail you might wish to have while actually out exploring the city. But the OpenStreetMap maps used directly are the tool I always rely upon.

The waterfront of the beach city of Warnemunde, as the ship sails in.

The small yacht harbor of Warnemunde

The boardwalk in Warnemunde

Taking the train from Warnemunde to Rostock

In the center of Old Town Rostock at the market square.

The main pedestrian shopping street of Rostock on a rainy afternoon

Rostock has become a thriving modern city

The Rostock area is famous for its strawberries in summer

THE PHYSICAL PLAN OF BERLIN: Berlin dates to the mid 15th century, but it did not become a significant city until the rise of the Prussian realm during the 17th century. Slowly King Frederick William II who was known as Frederick the Great expanded the city, adding important boulevards such as Unter den Linden and important public buildings and monuments. When Germany became a united country in 1870, the capital of the Kingdom of Prussia, which was Berlin, became capital of a united Germany. As political and economic power became consolidated here, the city grew into a great metropolis, a city of culture and vitality. As Germany became an industrial nation, Berlin became the hub of the country's railroad network and road system as well as an important industrial city in its own right.

Adolph Hitler had grand plans for the rebuilding of Berlin into a showplace of Nazi power. He had his chief architect Albert Speer develop master plans and models of a city that was going to be imposing through its monuments and public buildings, making it a model for the Nazi concept of autocratic rule of a united people. As the war deepened and bombs began to fall on the city, Hitler proclaimed that Berlin needed to be destroyed so it could be rebuilt. But the total destruction of the city at the final stage of the war, and the great loss of life that accompanied it was surely more than he had ever envisioned. As a part of the plan not only to rebuild Berlin, but to make Germany a strong country in which its military could move freely, the Nazi government did invent the Autobahn, or what are now called the Freeways or Interstate highways. And at one point early in his reign, he had a small car designed for the common folk, and in German, the name was Volkswagen – the people's car.

Berlin is once again the capital of a unified Germany. It has been totally rebuilt, especially the former Communist dominated east. With a metropolitan population of over 3,500,000 people, it is the largest city in Germany and the second largest city in the Baltic Sea region after St. Petersburg, Russia. The city spreads out along both banks of the River Spree in a flat to gently rolling landscape that exhibits a mix of broadleaf woodland and farms. It has a temperate summer weather pattern, but on occasion temperatures can reach the low mid 30's Celsius or 90's Fahrenheit. Winters are cold and there can be heavy accumulations of snow, but in recent years with global warming the winters have been less severe.

There is still a distinct difference between former West and East Berlin with regard to architecture and urban function. The former heart of prewar Berlin was the massive park known as the Great Tiergarten. The Brandenburg Gate at the eastern end of the park led to the beautiful tree lined boulevard known as Unter dem Linden. This area was the commercial heart of the city. But after the war came the division of Berlin into what would essentially become two cities.

West Berlin developed its own city center along the Kurfurstendam, a street that followed a northeast to southwest direction leading out from the Great Tiergarten. This became a glittering commercial street, and still is to this day. West Berlin was redeveloped with beautiful apartment blocks on tree-shaded streets interspersed with localized shopping areas. There was no regularized street pattern, and is not to this day, but the major boulevards do at least divide the area into large tracts. Few high-rise buildings were developed, the city keeping a relatively even profile.

And apart from local administration, this was not a capital city. Bonn had become the capital of West Germany since Berlin was behind the then known Iron Curtain, surrounded by Communist East Germany.

East Berlin became the official capital of the Democratic Republic of Germany, what the West simply called Communist East Germany. It was developed along Soviet lines with rather massive blocks of apartments and government buildings similar in design to those found in the Soviet Union -gray and drab. Many bombed out areas were simply cleared of rubble and left vacant. Overall East Berlin was a somber city with only a few streets fully developed in the Communist vernacular to showcase the so-called grandeur of the state system.

With the reunification of the country, Berlin became one city, but the West Berlin city center known as Kurfürstendamm was unable to provide space for all the new development. Most of the new construction has taken place in Mitte, the former city center district of East Berlin. Today there are in effect two great city centers in Berlin, each with its own distinct character. Mitte has seen massive redevelopment with modern high-rise apartment blocks, hotels and office buildings representing the latest in design. There is a vibrant downtown shopping area along Friedrichstraße that now rivals the Kurfurstendam in former West Berlin. A classic example of buildup in the east is Potsdamer Platz, a few blocks to the south of Friedrichstraße, which until 15 years ago was a vacant clearing, and today is a vibrant development of shops, offices and residences where several underground and above ground transport lines cross. Modern Berlin in effect has two downtown cores with the Great Tiergarten separating them. The Kurfurstendam architecturally represents the 1950's and 60's while Mitte is definitely 21st century.

Where once the Brandenburg Gate was behind the Berlin Wall erected by the Communists to keep the two cities apart, today it is the proud symbol of a united Berlin. And opposite the gate is the German Parliament, which once again serves as the heart of modern government. The Reichstag stands as a proud symbol of a united Germany. After it was set afire by Nazi forces before the war, it stood as a grim reminder of that terrible period in German history, and the Berlin Wall was immediately to its east.

Present day Berlin is considered to be a city-state within Germany, what Europeans would simply call a province. A Senate of eight members, the chief of which is the Regierender Bügermeister or mayor governs the city. The city government is housed in the Abgeordnetenhaus, or what in English would be a city hall. The city-state itself is divided into 12 boroughs, known in German as Bezirke. These are essentially self-governing neighborhoods, not unlike the boroughs of New York City or London. Each borough's mayor works in consort with the overall mayor who heads the city's senate as noted above. Although it is a massive city, Berlin is quite compact for its size, owing to the fact that most residents live in apartment blocks. Only in the outer suburbs will one find single-family housing. But despite this closeness, there are many green spaces and Berlin does not feel overly crowded.

Berlin's neighborhoods or boroughs are each quite distinctive. Before the Berlin

Wall came down, this was not only a divided city, but each side represented a different political system. East Berlin was capital of the German Democratic Republic. It was a rather grim city and contained many neighborhoods that were still partly destroyed from World War II. Only the principal streets showed any signs of modernization and vitality, but still with a measure of austerity. West Berlin was semi-autonomous as a city-state, but militarily supported by the United States, Britain and France. It recovered rapidly, sprouting modern apartment blocks, office towers and shopping centers. And East Berlin was guarded by Red Army troops from the Soviet Union.

Although Germany is a fairly homogenous country population wise, there has been immigration permitted for the purpose of filling factory jobs in the country's expanding industry. As a result, Berlin does have about 12 percent of its population comprised of Poles, Turks and other foreign nationals. This has caused some consternation and occasional violence against outsiders, especially against the Turkish populace. With the plans to house more refugees from Syria, Iraq, Afghanistan and eastern Africa, tensions and possible violence may flare in the future.

Once Berlin was home to one of the largest Jewish populations in Europe. Jews were an integral part of the city's business, medical and educational life, but Nazi persecutions and eventual exterminations destroyed this community. Today only a handful of Jews live in Berlin, a shadow of the once great community. Jews only account for .4% of the overall population, or some 14,000 people. But large numbers of Turkish and Polish workers have made their home in Berlin. They do live in self-segregated neighborhoods, partly because often choose not to culturally integrate into the nation. Some Germans criticize these immigrants as not meeting the national standards for cleanliness. These attitudes are not unlike those that Adolf Hitler used to fan the flames of resentment against the Jews and other non-Germans. However, today's German people are far more enlightened and such madness could not happen again. American, Canadian, Australian and British residents or visitors, on the other hand, are very welcome and treated with great kindness and respect. If one can speak a bit of German it makes the welcome that much greater. I am quite fluent in German and have found the people to be incredibly friendly and helpful.

WHAT TO SEE AND DO IN BERLIN: When coming to Berlin as a visitor there is much to see in both the eastern and western sectors so as to see the major redevelopment that has taken place in what was once behind the Berlin Wall. And there are major sites that are considered the hallmarks of the city's history. When your ship docks in Warnemunde, you will have various options with regard to the long trip to Berlin:

* Most cruise lines offer different Berlin itineraries, but all first involve getting to and returning from the city, which is over 200 kilometers or 130 miles away. The majority of cruise tours will be by motor coach and you can count upon approximately two hours of driving time each way. If the Autobahn is not crowded, the drive can be made in about one hour and 40 minutes.

* A few cruise lines charter a full train and then have motor coaches waiting at the Hauptbanhoff in Berlin for the various tours. The line from Warnemunde does not accommodate high-speed ICE trains, and thus the journey takes approximately three hours.

* Hiring a private car and driver/guide is my preferred option although costly. A car can make the journey in around 90 minutes under good conditions. And once in Berlin, a car is more maneuverable and can get you around the city to see and do more in the time allocated. I found that to charter a private car in Rostock on your own for the round trip to Berlin plus a day of sightseeing will cost as much or more than what the cruise line could arrange. It is also vital to keep in mind that if you charter a car and driver on your own and if for some reason you are delayed by traffic or other problems and return to the ship late, you may find that the ship will have sailed without you. However, if you have the cruise line make the arrangements, the ship is then obligated to wait for you no matter how long you are delayed. For this reason alone, it is best not to try and arrange a charter on your own.

* Some cruise lines offer transportation into the city and provide you with maps and information regarding a self-guided tour. I highly recommend against this option unless you have been to Berlin before. The city is too large and spread out and the public transport system too complex for a novice to accomplish much on his/her own. It simply will be a wasted day. But if you should choose this option, there are ways to get around the city far more effective than simply walking from where your transport from the ship brought you:

** The U Bahn and S Bahn - these are the two major systems of underground and above ground rapid transit. The two systems integrate to provide a multiplicity of routes around the city. Day passes can be purchased, but you need to study the map carefully to determine the best routes to use.

** Hop on hop off bus service - there are multiple routes and these busses can take you to most of the important sights that most visitors want to see. And there are narrations and maps provided.

The following descriptive list represents only the most major of Berlin's important monuments since your time will be limited (listed in alphabetical order):

* Alexanderplatz – This was the central business district of old East Berlin, but it has undergone westernization since reunification. It is here that the Berlin Tower is located. Shops here also maintain a variety of opening and closing hours.

*Alexander von Humboldt University - Located on Unter den Linden, this famous academic institution is where Albert Einstein once taught. It was also the site of the infamous Nazi book burning, memorialized in the university's central quadrangle.

* Berlin Television Tower – If the weather is clear, this is the best observation

platform from which to view the city. From the open-air deck one can have a 360-degree panorama of all Berlin from an observation deck 203 meters or 665 feet above the city street level. It is located at Alexanderplatz. However, the wait to ascend the tower can be over an hour if you have not purchased prior tickets. The tower is open daily from 10 AM to Midnight.

* Berlin Dom - This massive cathedral located along Unter den Linden is the largest of the Lutheran cathedrals in Berlin. Its organ is one of the largest in Europe and some of the up market cruise lines arrange for a brief organ recital during their visits to the cathedral. Guided tours are offered from 9 AM to 8 PM Monday thru Saturday and from Noon to 8 PM on Sunday.

* Brandenburg Gate – This is one of the city's most cherished monuments, standing at the end of Unter den Linden, the city's broad and once fashionable boulevard. The gate dates to the 18th century Prussian Empire, commissioned by Emperor Frederick Wilhelm II. It stood behind the Berlin Wall until the reunification of the city, and is now once again the symbol of Berlin. Cars may not drive through the gate. It is only open for pedestrian pass through, and it is considered a must do activity by all Berliners. The Emperor had it commissioned to commemorate the restoration of order following the Batavian Revolution, which occurred in The Netherlands. Prussian forces helped to restore order.

* Checkpoint Charlie – Once the most important crossing between allied West Berlin and Communist East Berlin. It is found at Friedrichstraße and Zimmerstraße, This is one of the most photographed venues in Berlin. Young actors dress in uniforms representing the American and East German guards and stand for photos during the day. The museum adjacent on Friedrichstraße #43-45 is open daily from 9 AM to 10 PM. At times there are people asking to stamp your passport with old stamps from the days when crossing the wall meant crossing a true border. But for most nations it is illegal to have what are now bogus stamps placed in your passport.

* East Side Gallery – This is the last surviving section of the Berlin Wall complete with its graffiti, now preserved in a park like setting, but standing in the exact spot where it once was part of the infamous wall. It is located at Mühlenstraße #3-100 and is open 24-hours daily.

* Gendarmenmarkt – The most beautiful of Berlin's public squares, graced by two of the city's major cathedrals and its concert hall. It is located in the heart of Mitte in former East Berlin. This is a major gathering place for people who take the Hop on Hop off bus around the city.

* Hakescher Markt – A district of small boutiques, cafes and galleries that once was the heart of the Jewish quarter of the city. It is located north of the River Spree on Rosenthaler Straße and shops maintain a variety of opening and closing hours.

* Holocaust Memorial – A stark reminder to the 6,000,000 murdered Jews of Europe, this memorial just opened in May 2005, and it is a reminder to the world

of what can happen under dictatorship gone astray. The memorial is located south of Unter den Linden and the Brandenburg Gate at Cora Berliner Straße #1 and open from 10 AM to 8 PM Tuesday thru Sunday. The memorial is closed Monday.

* Jewish Museum - Unlike the Holocaust Memorial, this museum provides a detailed history of the Jewish people in Germany as well as in the rest of Europe. It is located on Linden Straße #9-14 in former East Berlin. The museum is open from 10 AM to 8 PM daily, with extended hours to 10 PM on Monday. And tours are offered.

* Kurfürstendamm – This became the main commercial street of the western sector of Berlin. It is still the liveliest street in Berlin, brightly lit with neon at night. The bombed ruin of the Kaiser Wilhelm Memorial Church sits at the top end of the street as a symbol of the destruction wrought upon the city in 1945. Most shops on the Kurfurstendam do stay open late each night. The most important store is the massive Ka DaVe Department Store, an elegant shopping venue.

* New Synagogue – This reconstructed building once housed the largest Jewish congregation in all of Europe. The synagogue is just across the River Spree from Mitte on Oranienburger Straße # 28-30. The visitor center is open Monday thru Friday from 10 AM to 6 PM and on Sunday from 10 AM to 7 PM.

* Potsdamer Platz – This square was once used as a military parade ground. Today it is the heart of a maze of skyscrapers, representing the new face of Berlin. It is located just to the southeast of the Reichstag and is one of the examples of how former East Berlin has become so modern. It is an interesting and quite photogenic plaza surrounded by ultra-modern buildings. The S-Bahn and U-Bahn both can take you to Potsdamer Platz.

* Rathaus Schöneberg – The site of John F. Kennedy's famous "Ich bin ein Berliner" speech. It is the old town hall for the borough of Templehof that stood next to the former East Berlin Wall. It is appropriately located at what is now called John F. Kennedy Platz #1 and is open daily except Monday from 10 AM to 5 PM/

* Reichstag – The German Parliament has been fully restored and now serves as the legislative building for the nation. In 1933, it was burned, which gave Adolph Hitler the excuse he needed to declare himself as dictator. It stands at the eastern end of the Tiergarten and faces the Brandenburg Gate. Visitors are permitted to view the interior of the parliament from the glass dome above the legislative chamber. Guided tour of the building are also provided. Tours and visits to the dome are permitted from 8 AM to Midnight daily, but tickets must be purchased first. And there is relatively tight security upon entering the building. In my restaurant section, I will make special note of the Reichstag's elegant rooftop restaurant. You will need to show your passport at security if you visit the Reichstag.

* Schloss Charlottenburg – The largest of the surviving historical palaces in Berlin that date back to the glory of the Kingdom of Prussia. It was last home to Kaiser

Wilhelm II until the end of World War I. It is located in the suburban district of Charlottenburg to the west of the Kurfürstendamm. The palace is open and guided tours are offered between 10 AM and 6 PM Tuesday thru Sunday. The palace is closed on Monday.

* Tiergarten – The largest park in Berlin, the Tiergarten is a masterpiece in park design with its beautiful landscaping and numerous walking paths. The neighborhood to the north, also known as Tiergarten, became the middle-class sector of the city, housing academic and professional families.

* Topography of Terror – This museum located adjacent to the former Berlin Wall at Niederkirchnerstraße # 6 is dedicated to presenting the horrors of the former Nazi SS and gestapo through a series of photographic exhibits. It is quite graphic and disturbing, yet important in helping people understand what happened during that period of German history. It is open from 10 AM to 8 PM daily.

Berlin is a city that once was the center of culture for all Germany. After World War II, with the division of Germany by the victors, Berlin fell within the Soviet controlled zone that became the Democratic Republic of Germany. As noted previously, the city was not a part of East Germany, but rather divided among the allied powers and occupied up until German reunification. The eastern portion of the city became the capital of the austere and dictatorial regime of East Germany, and became separated from West Berlin by the infamous Berlin Wall. The capital of the Federal Republic of Germany, better known as West Germany, was located in Bonn and much of West German culture became rooted in Frankfurt or Munich. Once reunification was completed and Berlin became whole again, it once more became the national capital and the focus of importance. It is once again a city with a rich and vibrant nightlife, major symphony orchestras and many fine museums and galleries. Once again, Berlin has become the center for the German film industry and for its radio and television broadcasting. But Frankfort has remained as the financial hub of the nation. And Hamburg, as a port city, has developed as a major economic and cultural center. Berlin no longer has the star role among German cities.

DINING OUT: You will only have time for lunch during your one-day visit to Berlin. And on all of the organized tours, lunch will be provided so you will not have a choice of restaurants or a wide range of menu selections. Any visit to Berlin should become a gastronomic experience if you have the free time, which only a few of you will.

Like in Poland, the food of Germany is rich, substantial and very delicious. Roasted meats and chicken are served with crisp potato pancakes, sweet and sour red cabbage and washed down with heavy, dark beer. At lunch, Germans also like sausages and sauerkraut or fried veal or pork cutlet, known respectively as Wienerschnitzel or Schweineschnitzel. Spaetzle, small egg noodles covered in melted butter and parsley are a popular side dish.

For dessert, Germans love rich chocolate cakes with whipped cream and brandied fruits or crispy apple strudel or thin tortes made up of many layers of cake, nut fillings and butter cream icing. As a treat, marzipan candies are a popular snack. Marzipan is made from ground almond paste and has a most distinctive flavor, but many say it is an acquired taste.

If you are traveling to Berlin in a private car or going about on your own after arrival by either train or bus, I recommend the following few as possible venues for lunch because they best represent German cuisine at the midday meal (shown alphabetically):

* Boulevard Friedrichstraße – Located in Mitte at Friedrichstraße # 106c, this is a locally popular restaurant for traditional German cuisine at both lunch and dinner. It has a good reputation for consistent quality and a nice atmosphere with indoor or outdoor service. It is conveniently located in the former East Berlin downtown, close to many tourist venues. They are open daily from Noon to Midnight.

* Fassbender and Rausch - This famous chocolate shop also has an upstairs cafe where light meals are served for lunch since they open as early as 10 AM. The soup, sandwich and other light items give you the needed protein and energy that will then allow you to indulge in their decadent sweets. The shop and cafe are located at Charlottenstraße 60, just south of the Deutscher Dom in the Gendarmenkarket of former East Berlin.

* Gasthaus Kater Alex – Located west of the Kurfürstendamm shopping area, you will need to have your own car and driver or take a taxi to reach this gem of a restaurant. It is at Kaiser Friedrich Straße # 29. This is one of the finest restaurants serving traditional German cuisine in a superb atmosphere with impeccable service, one of the best dining establishments in the city. I highly recommend that you have the ship's concierge call to book a table. Their serving hours are Monday thru Wednesday from 9 AM to 10 PM, Thursday from 2 to 11 PM, Friday from 9 AM to 11 PM and Saturday from 2 to 11 PM.

* Happies - This is a small restaurant where the service and the quality of the food are hard to beat. Open from Noon to 8 PM, this is a good place to sample German cooking for lunch. It is located on Dunckerstraße 85 in the part of the city known as Prenslauer. It is not close to any of the main attractions, but worth taking a taxi just for lunch.

* Ka DaWe 6th Floor - This impressive restaurant will insure that you visit the famous Ka DaWe Department Store if for no other reason than to have lunch. The food is authentic and the selection is quite large. You can truly sample a taste of Germany in this one restaurant.

* Käfer Dachgarten-Restaurant - Located on the roof terrace of the Reichstag, or parliament building. Gourmet cuisine with a view out over Berlin is the hallmark of this unusual restaurant inside a national capitol building. Reservations are an absolute must and you will need to register in the lobby and be cleared by security before going up to the restaurant. To book a table go to their web page at

www.feinkost-kaefer.de a few days prior to your visit. The restaurant is open for breakfast and lunch from 9 AM to 4:30 PM and for dinner from 6:30 PM to Midnight.

SHOPPING: When going to Berlin for the day, generally on an organized tour, there is little or no time for shopping. Even if you are going on your own, there is so much to see that shopping become irrelevant other than buying a few souvenirs, which you will find available at most major scenic sights.

There is one major department store that will sometimes be included on tour itineraries, or that you can briefly visit on your own. Located on the Tauentzienstraße, the continuation of the Kurfürstendamm you will find KaDaWe, properly known as Kaufhaus des Westens. This is the Harrods of Berlin - the most upscale department store in the city. If you visit the Kurfurstendamm, this store is a must-see venue.

FINAL WORDS: The portions of Germany that were under the domination of the Communist regime have been fully integrated into a united nation. Scars of World War II and the grim architecture of the Communist Era are fast fading. Potsdamer Platz in Berlin is without exception the classic example of this transformation. Berlin is the most dynamic example of the strength of this reunification, and it is a city rich in history yet committed to building its 21st century image as a great European city. The pride of the city and of the entire nation is the Reichstag, the German Federal Parliament, which is located just west of the Brandenburg Gate. The Reichstag sat as a derelict building from the day it was ordered burned by Adolf Hitler until after the reunification of Germany. Millions of Deutschmark were spent to restore the building and once again it serves its original purpose. But more than just being a renovated building, it is a reminder of the tribulations of the nation from the end of World War I until the reunification in the ending years of the 20th century.

BERLIN MAPS

GREATER BERLIN

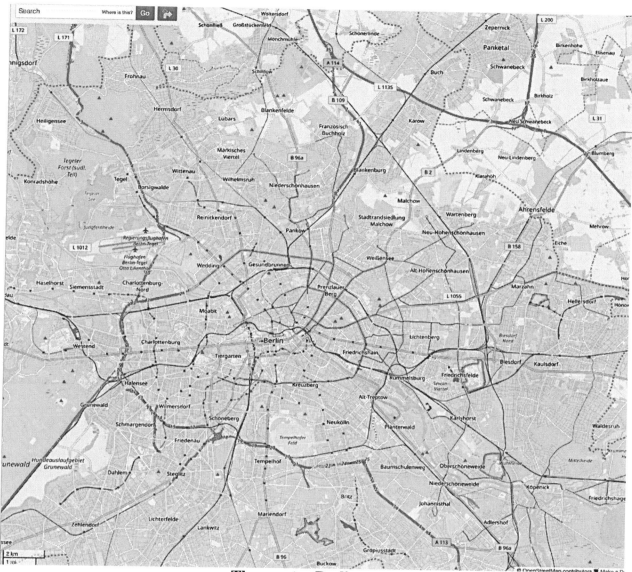

The greater Berlin area

This map is best viewed directly from OpenStreetMap.com on your personal device where it can be expanded or one specific area can be enlarged. Given the format of this book, it is impossible to display maps with the level of detail you might wish to have while actually out exploring the city. But the OpenStreetMap maps used directly are the tool I always rely upon.

THE TIERGARTEN

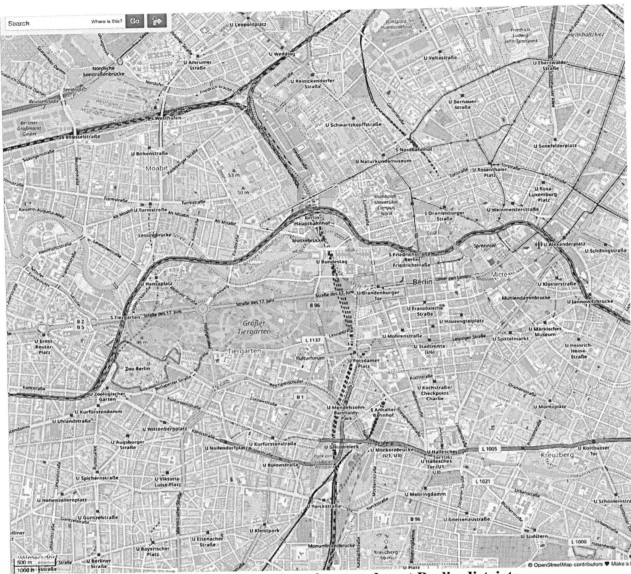

The Tiergarten – meeting of east and west Berlin districts

This map is best viewed directly from OpenStreetMap.com on your personal device where it can be expanded or one specific area can be enlarged. Given the format of this book, it is impossible to display maps with the level of detail you might wish to have while actually out exploring the city. But the OpenStreetMap maps used directly are the tool I always rely upon.

THE KURFURSTENDAM

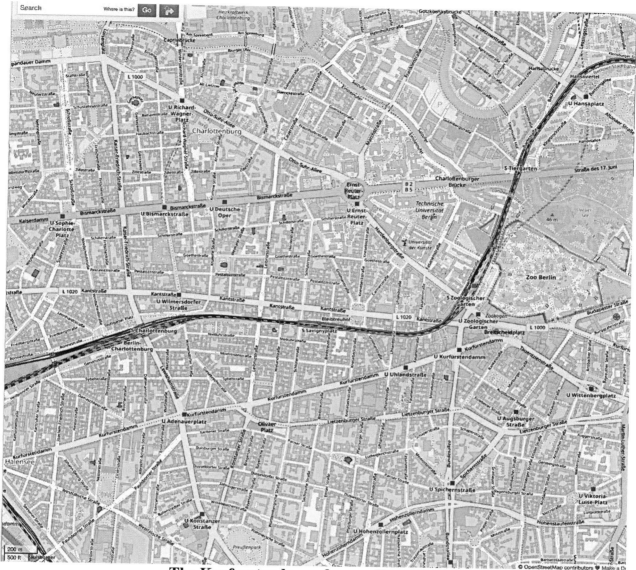

The Kurfurstendam – former West Berlin

This map is best viewed directly from OpenStreetMap.com on your personal device where it can be expanded or one specific area can be enlarged. Given the format of this book, it is impossible to display maps with the level of detail you might wish to have while actually out exploring the city. But the OpenStreetMap maps used directly are the tool I always rely upon.

MITTE

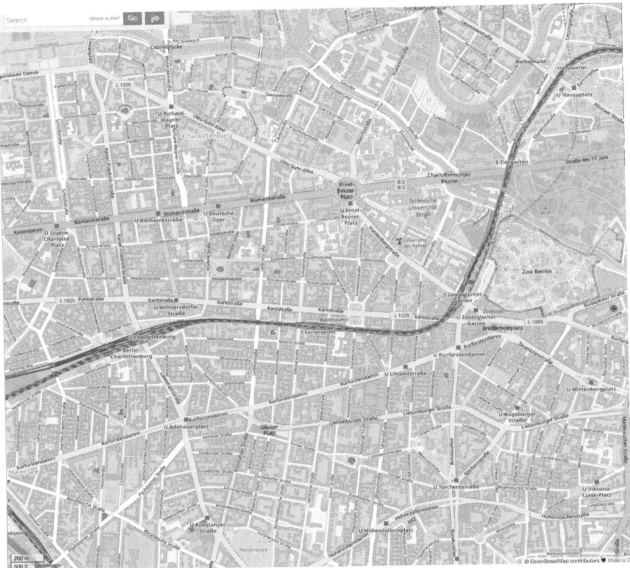

Mitte – heart of former East Berlin

This map is best viewed directly from OpenStreetMap.com on your personal device where it can be expanded or one specific area can be enlarged. Given the format of this book, it is impossible to display maps with the level of detail you might wish to have while actually out exploring the city. But the OpenStreetMap maps used directly are the tool I always rely upon.

A great aerial view looking over the heart of Berlin, (Work of Avda, www.avda-foto.de, per Wikimedia.org, CC BY SA 3.0)

A rooftop view over Berlin along the River Spree from the Reichstag

The Kurfürstendamm area was once the main hub of West Berlin

Ka Da We is the great Kurfürstendamm department store

Friedrich Straße is now the heart of former East Berlin's upmarket shopping

The Gendermarkt Platz in the heart of Mitte

The grand interior of the Berlin Dome (cathedral)

Germany's Reichstag once again functions as the national parliament.

The restored Brandenburg Gate

Alexander von Humboldt University where Einstein once taught

The new 21ˢᵗ century high-rises of former East Berlin

The Holocaust Memorial is in Mitte close to the former Berlin Wall

The Topography of Terror Museum's outdoor exhibits

Checkpoint Charlie once was the border between East and West Berlin

Souvenir military items from the former East Germany

The original sign showing entry into the Soviet Sector of East Berlin

ABOUT THE AUTHOR

Dr. Lew Deitch

I am a semi-retired professor of geography with over 46 years of teaching experience. During my distinguished career, I directed the Honors Program at Northern Arizona University and developed many programs relating to the study of contemporary world affairs. I am an honors graduate of The University of California, Los Angeles, earned my Master of Arts at The University of Arizona and completed my doctorate in geography at The University of New England in Australia. I am a globetrotter, having visited 96 countries on all continents except Antarctica. My primary focus is upon human landscapes, especially such topics as local architecture, foods, clothing and folk music. I am also a student of world politics and conflict.

I enjoy being in front of an audience, and have spoken to thousands of people at civic and professional organizations. I have been lecturing on board ships for a major five-star cruise line since 2008. I love to introduce people to exciting new places both by means of presenting vividly illustrated talks and through serving as a tour consultant for ports of call. I am also an avid writer, and for years I have written my own text books used in my university classes. Now I have turned my attention to writing travel companions, books that will introduce you to the country you are visiting, but not serving as a touring book like the major guides you find in all of the bookstores.

I also love languages, and my skills include a conversational knowledge of German, Russian and Spanish.

I am a dual Canadian-American holding both national passports. Apart from having lived in Canada, I also lived for a time in Australia. Arizona has been his permanent home since 1974. One exciting aspect of my life was the ten-year period, during which I volunteered my time as an Arizona Highway Patrol reserve trooper, working out on the streets and highways and also developing new safety and enforcement programs for use statewide. I presently live just outside of Phoenix in the beautiful resort city of Scottsdale.

TO CONTACT ME, PLEASE CHECK OUT MY WEB PAGE
FOR MORE INFORMATION AT:
http://www.doctorlew.com

Printed in Great Britain
by Amazon